Motivation from Animal Kingdom

Be the best animal

Parveen Sharma

Motivation From Animal Kingdom - *Be the best animal*
ISBN - 978-1-943851-58-4
Copyright © 2016 Parveen Sharma

No part of this publication may be reproduced, stored in a retrieval system, or transmitted, in any form or by means electronic, mechanical, photocopying, or otherwise, without prior written permission of the Author.

Requests for permission should be addressed to Parveen Sharma (contact@parveensharma.com).

Contents

Prologue

"If having a soul means being able to feel love and loyalty and gratitude, then animals are better off than a lot of humans."
—James Herriot

All mankind has descended from a single African mother. This is hard science and not a mythical flight of fantasy. Scientists have conclusively been able to prove that every single human being that inhabits the modern world is descended from a single female human being who resided 99000 to 100000 years ago in East Africa.

Judging by the tremendous diversity of the more than seven billion inhabitants of planet Earth, it hardly looks plausible. Who could imagine that a blonde blue-eyed Scandinavian male would share ancestry with a male or female member of the Zulu tribe in South Africa - yet it is true. Going back further into the mists of time, we will be amazed to find that the Chimpanzee and the modern man had a common ancestor. That would make them our cousins in a sense!

The truth of all life on earth is the fact that it has all descended from a common source of origin. From life at the microscopic level to that at the level of moss and lichen to the brightest of Harvard graduates, the beginnings are the same. Therefore to set man aside and on top of every other species is not only foolish and arrogant, but on a spiritual level –immoral too.

The way mankind, with all its perceived wisdom, is degrading the very environment in which it lives does nothing to prove its superiority.

On the contrary, man might one day be the cause of mass extinction of life on planet Earth as we know it. Life, of course, will return to planet Earth as it did on the previous five occasions when it faced mass extinction of life, but mankind will certainly not rise again.

So it is in our interest that we realize that all life on earth is inextricably linked - to the extent that every species has certain core strengths which the other could emulate. This is something that the rest of the animal kingdom is well-aware of and leverages for the benefit of their own species all the time. A leopard, for example, uses its spots to merge with the undergrowth in the jungle to benefit from the element of surprise that helps it flummox its prey.

A deer's tawny coat similarly helps it hide among bushes and scrub from any predators crouching nearby. The animal kingdom is replete with examples of animals not only coexisting but living in an active symbiotic relationship. Did you know that sharks, which are large species of fish, go to underwater cleaning stations where small fish such as wrasses and catfish give them a clean up? The latter do that by feeding on the parasites, mucous and dead tissue on the sharks' body. Not only do the sharks get a cleanup but they get tickled as well. This ensures that they are in too good a mood to make the smaller fish their meal.

Mankind too has long worked in close association with animals - with watch dogs and war horses, farm and milch animals and of course, pets. So it won't be far-fetched or weird to imagine that humans have imbibed many traits from animals. This may sound preposterous to modern man, but our ancestors had no compunction in being compared with animals, and sometimes even deified them.

In Hinduism, animals are the vehicles of Gods and Goddesses. Even few of the Gods are either half animals or animals themselves. Narasimha, the reincarnation of Lord Vishnu, has the torso of a lion and the lower body of a man. Lord Hanuman is the monkey God. The ancient Egyptians revered Anibus a jackal-headed God, and associated him with the afterlife. The Greeks considered Pegasus, a flying horse with wings divine.

Then there were mythical animals in European lore like dragons and unicorns which formed an important part of the local mythology there. The point being made here is that this chasm between mankind and other species which is so pronounced in present times was not so marked in the past. People would observe animals and learn and imbibe traits that they thought would be useful.

Even in modern times, the design of an aircraft was conceived by studying how birds are able to ride on drafts of air and how they execute a mid-air turn by banking. For all its scientific knowledge and prowess, mankind had to be humble and follow in the wake of a mere bird if it was to fulfill its long cherished dream of being able to fly.

This intimate study of animal behavior to learn lessons

that could help human beings themselves is something that has always been happening. Ancient Indians and Chinese developed various schools of martial arts by closely observing how animals moved and fought. We all know that many animals are stronger, faster and nimbler than human beings, and it certainly did us no harm in observing them and learning from them.

And we certainly did learn a lot from them. The bees taught us how honey is made; the beaver gave man the first lessons in dam building and the tiger showed what stalking and hunting are all about. Man in fact, of all the species relies far less on instinct and much more on learning from observation.

This is the reason why across cultures human beings' traits are often compared to the attributes of animals. That is why we have expressions like 'noble like a lion', 'sly as a fox', 'strong as an ox', 'gentle as a lamb', 'wise as an owl' (though in our culture an owl personifies stupidity!) and one could go on and on. The Chinese, more than any other people, with their millennia-old civilization recognized this very early and this is reflected in their zodiac signs named after animals like the rat, ox, tiger, rabbit, snake, dragon and so on.

It is my belief that the bonds that connect us with animals are subliminal and far deeper than we can imagine. There is something as to why the ancient cultures ascribed magical and mythical powers to them.

I believe that not only did God create all men and women equally, He created all creatures equally. Not just that, I feel that we are all spiritually linked to all of God's creations, and carry each other's traits in varying measures.

In the pages ahead, I will set out to explain how certain individuals possess a larger number of traits of a particular species or class. A man's behavior is the result of genetics and environmental influences. The latter comprise of not just human influences, but also that of the flora and fauna and certain cosmic influences.

Since
animals, especially mammals are the closest physiologically to humans, their influence is the most pronounced after that of humans themselves. When you go through the contents of the book, you will recognize the traits possessed by many of your kin, relatives, friends and possibly yourself.

The purpose of the book is to enlighten and entertain, while at the same time make us sensitive to the fact that life is not exclusive to human beings, and that we possibly share a lot in common with life forms we consider inferior.

Man and Tiger

The tiger has been feared, revered, and admired across civilisations from the oldest times. Both the Indian and Chinese traditions have many legends that bring to the fore many of the animal's known attributes. The tiger has been mentioned in Vedas, the holy books of the Hindus who also revere it as the vehicle of Goddess Durga.

Among the Chinese, the tiger is given the pride of place as one of the four mythical intelligent creatures; the other three being the dragon, phoenix, and tortoise. Given the aura of strength and even supernatural greatness surrounding the animal, it is not surprising that many individuals and institutions have liked to appropriate some of that glory, by associating themselves with the animal.

The legendary ruler of Mysore, Tipu Sultan used the tiger as a mascot and a royal emblem to express both his regal power and contempt for the British. He was appropriately called the Sher-a-Mysore or the Tiger of Mysore, for taking the fight to the heart of the enemy camp. Closer to our times, Sheikh Abdullah the Chief Minister of Jammu and Kashmir too was often referred to as the Sher-a Kashmir or Tiger of Kashmir, by the people of his state.

The Reserve Bank of India, which is the central bank of the country, chose it as its symbol. So important is the tiger in popular Indian imagination, that it is officially India's national animal. To many millions around the world, India is the land of tigers. So strong is the symbolism associated with the tiger that when Ang Lee, the renowned multi-academy award winner filmmaker, made a movie, *The Life of Pi* with Indian characters in it, one of the main protagonists in the movie was a Royal Bengal tiger called Richard Parker for some reason!

Part of the reason for man's eagerness to associate with the legend of the tiger may have to do with the fact that mankind has a hunter-predator past, as early man is known to have hunted and killed for food for hundreds of thousands of years. This primeval instinct which has been buried under centuries of relatively civilised living is somehow easily rekindled when one comes in some kind of contact with tigers themselves or their legends.

So what are those traits of a tiger that human beings so desire, which make them have no qualms about comparing themselves with a wild predator, which hunts and kills for food? The tiger symbolizes the epitome of strength, guile and ferocity - essential prerequisites for a successful predator. Then there is the element of stealth and mystery that makes the animal so intriguing. The tiger is known to stun its enemy by suddenly appearing out of nowhere, without having given any indication of its presence.

It is also known for its patience and endurance. It will stalk silently for a very long time if required and thinks nothing of traversing hundreds of kilometers. Who wouldn't want to have traits like those? These are the traits of a winner. Don't we see these in the achievers hailing from backgrounds as diverse as entertainment, politics, sports and the corporate world?

That's why the expression, *'he's a tiger,'* has become common currency everywhere.

Tiger, in fact, is quite a common nickname for people imagined to be dynamic or live wires. The animal denotes raw and regal power like nothing else. No wonder the Indian tiger is referred to as the Royal Bengal Tiger.

Tiger was the nickname given to Mansur Ali Khan Pataudi, the erstwhile Nawab of Pataudi, and flamboyant captain of the Indian cricket team. Senior Congress party leader and erstwhile Maharaja of the state of Jammu and Kashmir, Maharaja Karan Singh too shares the same honour.

The tiger's allure can also be explained by the fascination most people have with the dark and menacing nature of the beast. It is dangerous, unpredictable and sometimes pure evil - like when it turns man-eater. So there is always the fear of the unknown associated with the animal. The tiger exudes the same kind of magnetism that attracts young women to men with a rakish and even slightly unsavory reputation.

According to the Chinese horoscope, the tiger sign applies to people born in 1950, 1962, 1974, 1986, 1998 and 2010. A male born under this sun sign tends to procrastinate, but will be the first one to challenge the status quo, often by disruptive means. This may majorly impact his relationships, profession, and society as a whole.

Given to flashes of bad temper such a person is expected to do well as a leader of a political party, or someone who leads a social reforms movement. Money is never the main focus of his deeds and actions but is the inevitable result of his positive and affirmative actions.

Such men achieve a large measure of success in their lives with the forties being the age at which they really come into their own.

Similarly, women born in the Year of the Tiger will be dynamic and independent while possessing a natural flair for leadership. Her choice of mate has to be able to measure up to her own high standards. Because of the confident nature of her personality, she will be able to get along with men of any sign in the Chinese zodiac, but the long-term durability of the relationship would depend upon her mate's ability to match steps with her.

So close is the association of tigers with strength that seeing one in a dream denotes that one will be able to use one's strength, willpower and resilience to obliterate any challenges one might face in life. If the dream appears to be the kind that leaves you feeling positive, it is an indication of your being able to leverage your own tiger-like attributes to prevail over any situation.

On the other hand, a dream with a tiger in it giving you chase portends troublesome times for you. It signifies that you have suppressed anger or feelings towards some major issues in life, which if left unresolved could do you immense harm. This is more in the form of a warning nudge to use one's tiger-like abilities and seize initiative.

Of all the animals that human beings are compared to nothing gives more pleasure to people than being compared to a tiger.

Call someone a tiger and the chances are that their face will light up with a big smile, especially if it is a man being so addressed. William Blake, the famous English poet captured the majesty of the tiger in all its glory in his immortal poem, *The Tyger*. The stanza below captures the essence of the tiger's spirit.

> *Tyger Tyger burning bright,*
> *In the forests of the night:*
> *What immortal hand or eye,*
> *Dare frame thy fearful symmetry?*

What can we imbibe of the tiger's traits?

The Chinese zodiac may accord the pride of place to the tiger, but one needn't have been born in the year of the tiger to imbibe some of its traits that have led this regal animal to be so universally admired.

The tiger is the animal equivalent of a gentleman. For all his strength and aggression it does not attack without a reason. Jim Corbett, the great hunter turned conservationist of the last century, once passed a tiger as a small boy of eight or nine, and the animal just went away without attacking him.

Tigers also have an ingrained sense of fair-play which they display by eating only after the cubs and their mother have eaten – this comes from an animal that has to hunt down and kill other animals for its very survival.

Tigers often go for prey which is bigger than their size. That is why you often see tigers attack bears, rhinoceroses, and even elephants. Unlike lions, who hunt for pride, tigers' hunts are a solitary affair, with no help from any quarter. Even when its prey is heavier than itself, a tiger is able to outsmart it by using guile and intelligence. An ambush accompanied by a strategic attack on the neck of the larger animal usually does them in.

If we as human beings can be calm and humble in spite of being in a position of power, we would be hailed as the tigers among our peers. We should try and possess the grace and humility of the tiger to make allowances for those who are younger and weaker than us. In the case of men, a display of chivalry is a great trait to possess and always makes them stand out.

In today's dog eat dog world, fair-play is hardly ever on display. That is why we would rather address people as dogs, wolves and hyenas than tigers! Most people we know are busy putting others down, especially those who are in an inferior position to theirs. A tiger-like person, on the other hand, would never be proud of his or her strength but put it to good use for themselves and others.

If we are the kind of people who think nothing of taking on adversaries more powerful than ourselves or tackle seemingly insurmountable situations, we surely are tiger kind of people. By using our sharp thinking and adopting a strategic approach, we may, like the tiger outsmart any formidable opponent or obstacles.

Like the tiger, we should not be meek but venture way outside our comfort zone and use our intelligence and strategic vision to achieve beyond the limits that may have been prescribed for us. At the same time, if we can maintain a sense of calm and equanimity even when faced with a difficult situation, we would indeed be like the tiger - regal, super achievers and quietly confident.

The Hare and Us

The hare may have lost the race to the tortoise in the classical tale we have all read or heard; in reality, it is a much smarter creature. In Indian culture particularly, a hare is synonymous with cleverness. A hare with its piercing eyes minutely observing its surroundings and its twitching nostrils do come across as a naughty and terribly inquisitive animal, always up to some mischief. In Western culture, the popular modern narrative for hares has to be their tendency to attack vegetable patches and lay them bare.

In pre-Christian Europe, the Celts believed that a hare was the attendant spirit of the revered Goddess Eostre. In fact, the

Goddess was supposed to transform herself into a hare on a full moon night. Even the Buddhists link the moon with the hare, believing the former to be the shadow of the latter.

There is an old Chinese legend about Buddha asking for a representative from each species of animals to visit him before he departed from earth. Of the twelve that came to him, the hare was the fourth one to heed his call and was rewarded with the ability to rule over every fourth year in a cycle of twelve. According to the legend, children born in the year of the rabbit grow up to be intelligent, sensitive, graceful, loyal and merciful individuals but given to bouts of melancholy.

This seeming contradiction of the good with the maudlin or sad is a common refrain in folklore associated with hares. They are paradoxically considered pure and sinful, clever and foolish, brave as well as cowardly and pure and licentious at the same time.

An interesting legend from India about the hare points to its altruistic nature. Lord Buddha was a hare in a previous incarnation who along with an ape and a fox was approached by Lord Indra in the disguise of a beggar and asked to be fed. While the other animals were able to find him something to eat, the hare unable to do so jumped into fire, offering himself as meat. Pleased by his sacrifice, Lord Indra turned him into the hare-shaped mark that one sees on the moon on a full moon night.

The Greco-Roman tradition, on the other hand, does not attribute such noble traits to the hare. In it, the hare is associated with lust, romance, and fertility. Hares were, in fact, sacred to Aphrodite, the Goddess of beauty and magic, as they were supposed to possess the *gift of Aphrodite* or fertility!

So important did the ancient Egyptians consider the hare that they thought they had a role to play in creation as they symbolize both fertility and immortality. The Goth people of Europe, on the other hand, admired hares for their swiftness and considered them the very symbol of diligence and perseverance.

Hares, though similar to rabbits, are different in many ways. For one, they are larger and unlike rabbits that are born blind, newborn hares can take care of themselves just a few hours after being born. That points to how resilient and hardy they are. These are the facets of a hare's personality that appealed to people in ancient times when the linkages between man and nature were more real.

The ancients marveled at the speed, grace, and fertility of this clever animal while being wary of its, at times, mysterious nature. Like human beings, hares are a mixture of both the good and the bad with the former being more evident.

Hares at Play

The birds are gone to bed, the cows are still,
And sheep lie panting on each old mole-hill;
And underneath the willow's gray-green bough,
Like toil a-resting, lies the fallow plough.
The timid hares throw daylight fears away
On the lane's road to dust and dance and play,
Then dabble in the grain by naught deterred
To lick the dew-fall from the barley's beard;
Then out they sturt again and round the hill

Like happy thoughts dance, squat, and loiter still,
Till milking maidens in the early morn
Jingle their yokes and sturt them in the corn;
Through well-known beaten paths each nimbling hare
Sturts quick as fear, and seeks its hidden lair.

-John Clare (1793-1864)

What do we learn from hares?

People who take after the hare are supposed to appreciate the arts and mostly have a very sensitive disposition. At the same time, they want to reach for the stars and to this end, they keep themselves very fit and agile. The only thing that goes against them is their mercurial nature.

While not everybody is naturally endowed with hare-like traits, almost everyone can adopt some of their quite admirable traits to their own advantage. If one can have a sharp and inventive mind like that of a hare, one can turn around even a disadvantageous position to one that is beneficial.

One can aspire to be strong and fleet-footed like the hare and able to adjust to new situations in a jiffy, just like a newborn hare finds its bearings in a matter of hours. Likewise, fitness and the ability to persevere are those attributes of a hare that any person would do well to inculcate.

Then there is their legendary virility and fertility, something any man or woman would be happy to possess. Most people would possibly give a leg or an arm to be considered a manifestation of divinity. If you can manage to make people feel that you possess a divine energy, they would always treat you with deference, the way people in ancient times revered the hares. There is that certain element of the unknown, which is almost mystic in nature that hares came to signify in the past, and if any human being exudes that kind of an aura, they sure do have something in common with the hare.

Apart from the positives, there are certain negatives that a hare has, which one should positively abjure or avoid. Their moody and sometimes greedy nature often leads hares to the path of destruction. It would make sense for anyone to not inculcate such a trait in themselves. Hares are also sometimes looked upon as unreliable and treacherous to the extent of being seen as a bad role model to follow.

On the whole, however, the redeeming features outweigh the not-so-nice ones and this is something that most people would readily identify with. So the best course of action would be to imbibe and inculcate the hare's undoubtedly positive traits and attributes so as to become a stronger, more resolute, inventive and extremely intelligent individual.

The Elephant-Headed God

In Hindu culture, the invocation of Ganesha; the elephant-headed God is a necessary prerequisite to herald the launch of any new initiative or venture. So auspicious is the mere mention of his name that he is invoked on occasions as disparate as the purchase of a new car, the entry into a new home, the birth of an offspring, somebody's marriage, the inauguration of a factory and so on.

To those not familiar with the immense love and affection with which Ganesha is regarded in India, the sheer scale of his popularity might appear very difficult to understand. But one look at any idol or painting of the merry-looking elephant-headed God with a pot belly and a merry twinkle in his eye, his short trunk turned to one side, would give the most die-hard skeptic a glimpse into the reasons behind this.

Ganesha is a friend, philosopher, and protector, all rolled into one. You love him, revere him or pray to him, but you are never afraid of him. He is like everyone's Santa Clause - children, grown-ups, male and female. Because of this love for Ganesha, elephants are amongst the most loved and admired animals in India. In spite of their huge size and enormous strength, people are well-disposed towards them. They are used in temple ceremonies, state occasions and often to give people a ride at fairs and festivals.

Elephants are also viewed with great reverence in the other great continent that they are found - Africa. In fact, the word for elephant in the African languages of Zulu, Tsonga, and Tswana means the same thing - the forceful or the unstoppable one. The Zulu people go a step further and revere the elephant not as a God, but as a Holy animal like the cow is for Hindus.

Just like in India where an elephant is said to embody positive traits; in African myth too elephants are the very epitome of decency to the extent that they are often thought to exhibit kindness even to those who would deceive them. According to the legends of the Wachaga people of Tanzania, the elephant used to be human once, but treachery made it lose all its limbs, save the right arm which now serves as the trunk.

The recurring theme in elephant lore around the world is one of nobility and grace combined with enormous strength. The latter was in ample evidence when Hannibal stunned the ancient Romans when he descended upon them from the Alps in the company of his war elephants. In India too, elephants have been an important instrument of war since times immemorial. There is mention of their use in the Hindu epic Mahabharata, and the Greeks have left accounts of the use of war elephants in the famous battle between Alexander the Great and the Indian king Porus.

In the last century, elephants were also extensively used in the lumbering industry to help carry enormous loads of felled trees in the thick tropical jungles of North East India and Burma. The British also used them in their many tiger hunts in the Indian jungles. The process involved their brave hunters clambering on to a platform known as *howdah* on the back of the elephant and shooting at the poor tigers from their safe vantage points!

The popularity of elephants has a lot to do with the fact that these magnificent beasts bond wonderfully well with humans and willingly obey instructions of their puny handlers whom they could easily squash like a fly. Tellingly, the handlers or mahouts as they are called in India have a very personal relationship with their charges. The elephant yields to the mahout not because it fears, but because it has an emotional bond with it.

In the wild too elephants are a social lot living in herds and displaying an acute sense of loyalty to one of their own. Elephants are known to attack trains if one of their members gets run over by accident. They are also known to grieve for days for their dead and even forego food, much like we humans do.

Is it any surprise that elephants are an important part of modern animal lore with many movies and comic books featuring the elephant as an important protagonist? Think Tarzan movies and comics, the popular Hindi movie classic *Hathi Mere Sathi* and many others that come to mind.

"A king who always cares for the elephants like his own sons is always victorious & will enjoy the friendship of the celestial world after death." **-Chanakya**

What can we learn from elephants?

The question really should be what can't we learn from elephants? They are noble and caring while being immensely strong. While afraid of no creature that walks the earth, they are willing to be great friends with man, a creature much weaker than themselves.

They love their families to death and always seek to protect them from danger. Their sociability is as legendary as their strength. When it comes to the crunch, there is no foe as fearsome as the elephant. Its strength, of course, is humongous - it can uproot a tree with its trunk or squash a man's head under its massive foot like it were a bag of tomatoes. Yet it is playful and enjoys frolicking in water!

Aren't these the properties that a perfect person would have? To be noble and immensely caring and not making a great show of one's strength, reaching out to those that are weaker than you, looking after your family, being immensely sociable, having equally the ability to pulverize any enemy and be playful as a child when required -these are the traits that anybody would be too happy to possess.

Elephants embody the best traits that any human can aspire to possess. Their innate sense of empathy and a sense of themselves as socially responsible individuals along with their ability to find joy in the daily business of living makes them among God's most evolved creatures.

They are so like us in many ways. They have a similar life span, love and nurture their families like we do and feel intense grief the death of their near ones. Like us, they are very individualistic yet able to function quite effectively as part of a group.

In compassion, they sometimes go a step ahead than humans in that they extend their kindness to members of other species. They are no fair weather friends and will always support their friends in times of adversity. So in many ways it is far easier for humans to identify with elephants than any other animal, with possibly the exception of the whale, which too has a much evolved social behavior pattern.

Anyone who aspires to be like the elephant will find it easy to do so. All that one needs to do is to hold on to the finest human traits and hone them some more. It would, of course, be impossible to replicate the amazing hearing ability of elephants who hear sounds we never can, but having a finely developed sense of hearing would do us a world of good. That is equally true of possessing a memory like that of an elephant, who can remember for a lifetime!

Be like a Bear

For the many children and even adults around the world, who have had the pleasure of being acquainted with *Balloo the bear*, the much loved and adored character in Rudyard Kipling's Jungle Book, a bear embodies the wisdom of all times! This totally adorable character was made even more famous by the many movie and television adaptations of this gem of a book.

Balloo the bear guiding the orphaned human kid *Mougli* in the ways of the jungle and keeping him away from his arch enemy, *Sher Khan* the tiger, made for a fascinating as well as a heart-warming story that touched all. Bears are found in different shapes and sizes and in different parts of the world.

India has three species of bears, the formidable Black and Brown bears of the Himalaya region and the Sloth Bear found extensively throughout the country.

The North American bears like the Grizzly Bear and the Polar Bear are creatures of enormous size and a fearsome site to behold from up-close. Two of the loveliest bears that exist are to be found in China and Australia. While the former is home to the gentle Giant Panda, Australia is the place where the cuddly Koala Bear is found. Both these pretty looking animals are used extensively as part of the cultural imagery of their respective host nations.

Prehistorically, bears were an important part of religious cults followed by fishing and hunting tribes that lived in ancient Finland and Siberia. The early Chinese people too worshipped bears while Korean mythology identifies the bear as the ancestor of their people. Bears form an important part of the Indian American folklore as well. Most tribes ascribe mystical and medicinal properties to a bear and references to bears are an important part of many religious ceremonies.

Though one might not think so, going by their bulky nature and reputation of being solitary predators, bears are a highly social animal. They exhibit a commendable amount of intelligence comparable to higher animals like chimpanzees and human beings. Bears are known to lay a tree trunk across a river to help it cross without swimming.

Mother bears almost replicate the behavior of a human mother in that they display tremendous tenderness towards their cubs whom they can both shower with affection and provide a reprimand when required. Cubs and older bears observe a complex code of social behavior to help them forge relationships and help them distinguish a friendly individual from a dangerous one.

Bears not only have an extremely well-developed sense of smell, they can hear even the lowest of frequencies like dogs. Like human beings they can see in color and their vision is almost as good as ours. Besides that, they can move really fast, going at speeds of sixty kilometers per hour. No wonder it is foolhardy to make a bear angry!

Bears, like most human beings, are omnivorous and can eat roots, tubers, fruits, insects, fish, rodents and if need be even from a garbage dump. This wide range of diet allows them to gain their massive bulk, which they need to help them last the time they spend hibernating in winter when food is very difficult to come by.

Look for the bare necessities
The simple bare necessities
Forget about your worries and your strife!
The bare necessities are Mother Nature's recipes
That bring the bare necessities of life

-Balloo the bear in Jungle Book

Bears and us

Bears do have a fascinating persona and many are the traits that human beings can imbibe from these magnificent creatures. Like the bear, one can be a very powerful person who does not make a show of one's strength, but when provoked reveals a dangerous and formidable a foe.

A person with a bear-like personality will have no intention of needlessly messing with anyone, but should you try to make inroads into their turf, or try to take away what is genuinely theirs, they will come charging to protect and secure what is theirs. Like a bear, one may not always display a great show of one's emotions, but one would know one's priorities in life, and there would be hell to pay for anyone who tries to jeopardize what is important to them - for instance, one's children or livelihood.

There are people who, like a bear, would like to do nothing better than curl up and sleep for long hours. The bears hibernate in winter months when the food supply is low to conserve energy. While this may not be true of many human beings who oversleep because of laziness, there are those who, like hibernating bears, are able to prepare for bad times. They don't hibernate of course but are more resourceful in being able to deal with emergencies.

A bear-like person will be a doer and an achiever. Like a bear who has to use his or her inventiveness to procure the vast amount of food it needs to support its build, a human being who has a never-say-die attitude that makes him or her battle immense odds and persevere in achieving their objectives in life is indeed a winner.

A bear-like individual will never really be required to use all of his or her formidable faculties, be it physical or mental to deal with the task at hand. Like a bear who merely extends his paw to pluck a fish out of the water, this kind of individual will get what he wants without the slightest of show or fuss.

Such people can easily assume a leadership situation in any large organization by the ability to achieve seemingly daunting objectives in the most matter of fact way. They would never seek confrontation, but if challenged never ever back off. On the contrary, they would give it their all to get the desired end.

Another trait that makes them a great asset to any team is their instinct to nurture and protect their own. The expression bear-hug has probably come from this. Don't we all love big cuddly bear-like figures because of the sense of security that they give us? Santa Clause would probably not be half as popular as he is with children, but for his big bear-like girth and bearing.

There is something to be said about the bear - this very unique and awe-inspiring creation of God is a fearsome beast with an awe-inspiring physicality, yet industrious, dexterous and playful by turns. There is much to admire, learn and indeed inculcate from these magnificent animals.

Mother Cow

If ever an animal were to be associated with the soul of a civilization, it has to be the cow in its association with the Hindu civilization. Long venerated as Mother Cow or *gau mata*, because of its gifts of milk and allied products, male offspring to help plough the land, and dung to fertilize the soil and burn as cooking fuel in the kitchen, the cow has been at the center of India's primarily pastoral economy for millennia.

It is not surprising that it has the pride of place among all animals in the Hindu society with even its urine being consumed as part of a major religious ritual. Nowhere else in the world are cows the object of deification that these bovine animals are in India among the Hindus. But these do form an important part of the folklore of other countries as well.

It is, for example, believed in the English countryside that if one sees a herd of cows sitting in a field, imminent rain is on the cards! According to the ancient Egyptians, the sky is a gigantic cow and the sun is its calf. A heavenly cow has also been mentioned in ancient African and Scandinavian legends.

The most striking thing about cows, if one were to take the trouble of observing them, is that they always appear to be placid, unruffled and calm. Normally one would not associate aggression with them. In India, the cow is a metaphor for a docile person. But there is far more to the humble cow than meets the eyes.

People like cowherds who deal with these animals on a daily basis know that cows are so much like people - every individual has its own traits. A cow can be friendly or cantankerous, stubborn or docile, aggressive or affectionate, depending upon how it is disposed on a particular day.

Like human beings, there will be cows who are bullies and there will be those that are docile. While they will be afraid of new experiences, they will still be attracted to them, as they are a curious species, much like human beings themselves.

However, overriding all their other traits, it is the gentleness of cows that is the most prominent. No one ever feels intimidated in a cow's presence. According to Mahatma Gandhi, cows are a *poem of compassion.* At the same time, they have many other traits that point to their level of intelligence and their basically inquisitive nature.

They form lasting friendships with individuals they get along with and like us, have mood swings with things like gloomy weather depressing them and bright weather perking them up. They even hold lifelong grudges against other cows who have rubbed them the wrong way. Then there are those cows who are the leaders of a group and any new entrant will have to take time to network and get accepted by the herd.

Not surprisingly perhaps, cows are as forgiving as they are affectionate, even to those who haven't been good to them. Is it any wonder that cows are universally looked upon as basically gentle and benevolent animals, who would only do you good?

In the Chinese zodiac, the people born in the years 1901, 1913, 1925, 1937, 1949, 1961, 1973, 1985, 1997 and 2009 fall under the astrological sign of the cow. Apparently such people are very lucky with their jobs, and should, therefore, choose an appropriate career path for themselves that does not involve setting up a business. Their prospects for love as well as health, however, are not so bright and they should exercise due caution there!

What we can learn from cows

Unlike many other animals that awe or intimidate us with the special prowess that they are endowed with, cows teach us to be ourselves. They make no demands from us in wanting to inspire us to be extraordinary or super-achievers. On the contrary, they nourish us by providing us with milk to drink.

What we can learn from cows is to get in touch with our intrinsic nature and not try to be someone that we are not. We have to be comfortable in our own skin and learn to be content and live in peace. Like the cows, we can be gentle and non-threatening towards people yet possess our own idiosyncrasies in full measure.

We have to navigate life with all its myriad joys, travails, awkward and sometimes dangerous situations, taking the rough with the smooth in our stride, while not for once losing one's equanimity. Immense love for one's offspring is again something that we share with cows, and seeing them take up cudgels on behalf of their calves is inspirational and would motivate us to look after our own offspring.

If we can, like the cow, feel affection easily for all, even towards those who have not been all that great towards us in the past, our lives would be that much happier and practically stress-free - much like the idyllic life of farm cows grazing on grass in the lush and serene countryside. Perhaps that is the reason why the great Hindu God, Krishna chose the life of a cowherd, someone who liked nothing more than playing his flute while tending to his cows on the grassy banks of the river Yamuna.

In today's fast-paced times where one is constantly racing against deadlines, things like empathy and consideration for other people's feelings are often not a top priority for most people. This leads to a whole lot of angst and unnecessary hostility. If we could all take a leaf from the cow's book and inculcate the humane and gentle aspects of our personality, instead of forever being driven by aggression, the world would become a much happier place.

The cow is but an animal, who shows the magnanimity and

sagacity that is beyond most humans. This speaks volumes about how misplaced our sense of superiority over other animals is. Our ancestors were aware of it and in their wisdom, they gave the cow the most exalted of statuses - that of a mother.

Faithful like a Dog.

There is not even a shadow of doubt that of all the animals that abound in God's world, the closest any has come to being regarded as family by humans is a dog. To those who love dogs, their being family is not a question, it is a fact of life. We have all heard stories about how eccentric billionaires bequeath their millions to their dogs whom they designate as heirs; or of the Indian royalty of yore who would hold grand weddings for their dogs to which they invited other royals from around the country!

Even those less endowed with wealth would think nothing

about splurging on expensive kennels, bejeweled collars and gourmet dog food for their precious pets. There are those who share a bed with their dogs and pretty much give them the run of the house.

What is it about dogs that attracts us to them in this so personally emotional way? Ask any dog lover, and they will give you a long list of reasons. Dogs are ever faithful, will love you come what may, will guard you come what may and they are such delightful company, they will say. They will then go on to relate their favorite and legendary dog tales - someone's dog guarded his or her grave for days after the poor soul departed, how an old man who had a heart attack was saved by his dog, because it pressed the speed dial for an ambulance and so on and so forth.

But why is there such an amazing bond between dogs and mankind, as so many of these fantastic but true stories show us? There is a theory which suggests that dog faces are like human baby faces -adorable and cute. While human babies grow up and lose their innocent charm, dog faces are such that they always look adorable! The other more plausible explanation which has its basis in science seeks to find an answer to how this bond evolved.

Dogs are basically evolved from wolves and in the early days of man when humans lived in caves, a sort of a bond formed between wild dogs and early man. The former warned the latter of ever present danger from wild animals or rivals and this favor was returned by man by providing food to the helpful dogs. Over millennia, this bond grew much stronger and personal.

But what about the extraordinary love, affection and

devotion showed by dogs to their masters? The scientific explanation for this is that dogs in the wild unhesitatingly look up to the leader of the pack for their survival and this behavior is replicated in modern human homes - they look upon their masters in the same way. This means that they are programmed by instinct to behave in their tremendously loyal fashion to ensure their own survival and well-being!

That being said, there is no doubt about the fact that the bond between dogs and humans is an extraordinary one and has no parallel in any other example of inter-species interface. There is a famous story from the Indian epic Mahabharata where the righteous king Yudhishtra refused to enter heaven because the gatekeeper wouldn't allow his faithful fellow traveler a dog, a place in heaven. On hearing this, the dog, none other than the God of Death himself, who had taken up that form to test for Yudhistra, blessed the good king and welcomed him to heaven.

Dogs have been an integral part of Greek folklore, as well as that of other parts of Europe. Their ability to assist in the hunt not only made them valuable companions but also spawned many legends of mystical dogs involved in the hunt. This is particularly true of the Wales region of the present day United Kingdom.

"A dog is the only thing on earth that loves you more than he loves himself."

—*Josh Billings* (a.k.a. Henry Wheeler Shaw; humorist and lecturer)

Dogs and us

What is there to not like about dogs and who wouldn't like to possess the sterling qualities of a dog? If the ability to love selflessly, show unstinted devotion, putting the safety of your companion before your own and at the same time show a childlike zest for life at all occasions makes one a dog person, then let's have more and more dog persons in this world.

There are these famous run-ins between dog persons and cat persons, with each category of the person being absolutely sure that they are the better lot. The clinching argument often presented by dog people is that like their pets, they are loving family people unlike the owners of cats who are impervious, selfish and self-centered like their pets.

The fact that there are more dog people than cat people probably says something about the truth of the above assertion. There is really so much about a dog that is admirable. They are so energetic and resilient, and there is never a dull moment around them.

They are innately social and like to be among people and quickly make themselves the center of attraction. It may be that their relatively short life spans make them want to live their lives to the fullest, but this sure is an admirable way of living life - something that we can all learn from.

A dog's faithfulness is legendary and it probably surpasses that between close relatives. One has a sneaking suspicion that but for social conventions, many people would easily choose their dogs over a relative, should they be given the choice! If one can inculcate just a fraction of devotion and faith a dog shows towards its companion, one would earn the undying love and affection of the recipient for sure.

In all the talk about a dog's affable nature, one should not forget that dogs are incredibly brave as well. Not only are they superb as watchdogs, these animals are used by security forces to help unravel crime and sniff out explosives. If we as people could be equally courageous in difficult circumstances, we would be able to claim one more admirable attribute of a dog person.

Above everything else is the amazing love that a dog is capable of showing that is so mesmerizing and so worthy of emulation. In wanting to be a dog-like person, a human being would not have to take a leap of imagination, as we consider them a part of us. Like we do amongst ourselves, we give them their own personal names. Truly all of us are dog people somewhere deep inside, even if we have never owned a dog in our lives.

Say Meow

We all know that there are dog people and there are cat people and the two neither see eye to eye nor agree on anything except one - the love for their respective pets. The love that dog people have for their favorite species has been explained above. Now let's peep on the other side of the fence and look at what the cat people have to submit.

What's the first thing that comes to mind when you think of cats - temperamental, mercurial, individualistic, regal and graceful, but certainly not ever eager to please like a dog?

Unlike their canine counterparts, cats come with personality-loads of it! A cat as a pet will show affection for its master; not when they demand it, but when it so feels like and that too not for very long.

You would be a very optimistic cat owner indeed, if you expected your animal to be grateful for anything you do for it. Forget that it will watch over your house or be of any kind of use to you. If it so feels like, it may condescend to acknowledge your presence by momentarily rubbing its body against your leg; but beyond that it is happy to live its own life and expects you to get on with yours.

It is not that a cat does not harbor any love or affection towards those that are a part of its life, but it does not like to display it with boisterousness. It would much rather prefer that it be understood. It's like the cat is turning around and saying, "What's the fuss about Mister or Miss? You are family and I love you, but do I have to shout it from the rooftops every time I see you?"

Curiosity is one of the cat's defining traits, as exemplified in the classical adage, *curiosity killed the cat!* Then there is another classical association of cats with balls of yarn, with the animal constantly getting caught in tangles of wool-thread while trying to play some highly improvised games. The famous comic character Garfield typifies this mischievous, curious and playful nature of cats.

Fun and games aside, it would be wise to remember that the cats are essentially hunters and carnivores and include some rather large and ferocious members like tigers, lions, and leopards. They all come equipped with sharp retractable claws and their instincts are honed for the hunt and survival. Cats possess superb night vision and the sight of the animal in action at night with its eyes all aglow is something to behold.

These are stealthy and solitary hunters known to exhibit tremendous grace in their physical movement. With not a single wasted or superfluous move, they are fluid poetry in motion and this feline grace sets them apart in the animal kingdom. What also sets them apart is their fastidiousness about cleanliness.

Cats have been an integral part of the folklore of many cultures. The ancient Egyptians believed that cats captured the light of the setting suns in their eyes thereby keeping it safe till the next morning. That was why it was unlawful for common people to kill cats.

Similarly, the ancient Scandinavian Goddess Freyja reputedly rode in a chariot drawn by cats. This encouraged local farmers to leave offerings for the latter so as to curry favor with the Goddess and ensure a good harvest. There are many superstitions attached to cats as well, with many people considering a cat crossing their path as being inauspicious. In America, many people associate black acts with witches, whereas in England such cats are considered lucky.

Cats, of course, are a very popular pet the world over and many attribute this to the pretty appearance of the animal, with its shiny coat and aristocratic appearance. This is generally true of the expensive breeds of cat like the Siamese. But the most famous of all the cat characters has to be the smiling Cheshire cat immortalized by Lewis Carroll in his classic book for children and adults alike, Alice in Wonderland.

"You see a dog growls when it's angry, and wags its tail when it's pleased. Now I growl when I'm pleased, and wag my tail when I'm angry.
-The Cheshire Cat in Lewis Carroll's Alice in Wonderland

Be a cool cat

The very expression 'cool cat' is a give-away about what comes to mind when most people think of cats. These are cool customers, and who wouldn't like to be one or at least considered one. Cats are known to be individualistic, fastidiously clean and not the ones given to exhibitionism. Now which man or woman wouldn't want to be like that?

Then there are other traits that these stately animals possess like beauty, superb hunting skills and an innate sense of curiosity which makes it want to investigate and get to the bottom of things. Most of us would gladly wish to possess these traits as well.

Possibly the most impressive of the traits that cats possess pertain to their disposition. They never demand attention but command it. Whenever a cat walks into one's presence, there is a palpable energy that emanates from it, even though it does not prance around like a dog does. The very way a cat walks is a picture of grace and elegance. All of the above are the traits that humans could pick up from cats to their own benefit.

Cats teach you to never be frivolous and invest the time to know somebody well. That's why not everyone likes to keep cats as pets. They almost appear aloof and are mysterious in their ways. Yet if one were to look beyond the veneer and make an effort to know the animal, one would find that the cat makes a wonderful companion, who is intelligent and affectionate in its own way.

If as humans we encourage others to know the real person behind the façade we put up for the world, we would be able to make friends for life. Let's not share all our cards up-front, but invest our persona with some allure and mystery, so that the other person takes a genuine interest in knowing who we truly are.

If we can look after a cat quite well, we'll be able to take better care of our children. For they too like cats haven't been created to please us or dance to our tune (as dogs do), but to become complete individuals in their own right, who learn to love us for what we are, and not because they have to.

What a Bull!

Since the beginning of time, a bull has been associated with resilience, doggedness, determination and of course virility. Make no mistakes about this animal. It's a male and its masculinity defines it. This all-pervasive perception of power that this animal radiates probably led to many ancient cultures venerating it.

The bull was worshipped by the ancient Egyptians, Romans, Greeks, Mesopotamians, and the Celtic people. Because it personified virility, fertility and wealth, it came to be associated with positivity thus becoming an icon for many cultures. The 5000-year-old Indus Valley Civilization used to put its image on official seals. This trend continues in modern times as well, with the image of the bull signifying a buoyant stock market.

The bull is also used to depict the Taurus sun sign in the study of astrology. Predictably men born under the Taurus sun sign are pretty astute when it comes to money matters! So whoever chose the bull as a symbol for an ascendant stock market, knew what he was talking about.

A bull is supposed to be a very aggressive animal and this is not surprising considering its size. A fully grown male may grow up to be between 500 to 1000 kilograms in weight - a veritable battle tank! As they can be aggressive, the people handling them need to be very careful, as there have been a large number of human injuries worldwide attributed to bulls not being handled properly by their keepers!

It is this typically aggressive behavior which probably led to their being used in bull fighting, a tradition famous not just in Spain, but in South America, the US, and some Indian states as well. Another popular Spanish sport associated with the bull is the famous running of the bull festival in which brave young men run in front of the charging bulls. This was shown to Indian audiences in the popular Hindi movie *Zindagi Na Milley Dobara* a few years back. India, of course, has been holding bull races in the rural areas since times immemorial.

The bull has long been a part of the Indian civilization from very ancient times and this tradition continues till today. Bulls continue to be used by many poor Indian farmers to till the land and one will still find bullock-carts being used to transport people and goods in many parts of the 21st century India. The bull Nandi is the mount of the Hindu God Shiva, and its statues find a pride of place in all temples dedicated to the deity.

In Greek legend, the God Zeus took on the shape of a bull to woo the beautiful Europa. In ancient Sumeria and indeed among the many ancient tribes that roamed the Middle East, the bull was a symbol of protection and its statues often adorned the entrances to temples.

In modern times, it is not just the bourses that resonate with the power of the bull. Equally the basketball stadia of the US reverberate with the cheering of the audience when the famous Chicago Bulls team goes on a scoring rampage. Similarly the icon for the University of Texas, Austin football team is also a bull.

The bull and us

What is it that the bull has, that we would want to have? Quite a bit, it would seem. The young men would like to be both virile and strong like the bull while the older gentlemen would like to possess its doggedness, determination, and stamina to last the course.

The punters would, of course, want the bull-run to continue indefinitely in their lives. The ladies would appreciate the fact that the bull is a symbol of fertility and that is one trait they would definitely want to possess. The bull is an incredibly strong, powerful and aggressive animal, and these are the traits most men instinctively identify with. So any man worth his salt will at some point want to be identified with a bull in full flow.

Then there is that adage, *taking a bull by the horns*, signifying one's ability to grapple with the core of an issue, alluding to the fact that it may require guts equivalent to subduing a bull. Another example of the raw power associated with bulls is that the most popular energy drink in the world is called, what else, Red Bull!

One of the most outstanding movie characters played in cinema is that of a raging, out of control boxer portrayed by none other than the brilliant Robert De Niro in the twentieth-century masterpiece, The Raging Bull! Why the bull is also the symbol of the beast of a sports car, the Lamborghini! Truly there is no getting away from the imagery of a bull. It defines the male of the human species.

Whales - the empathetic mammals extraordinaire

In many ways, whales are an anomaly of nature - enormously large mammals that breathe with their lungs even though they live their lives in the deep seas among creatures far better adapted to that environment. Unlike other aquatic animals, the whales can't breathe underwater and need to periodically surface to get in the life-sustaining air. Very unlike the other cold blooded creatures of the seas, the whales procreate like us with mothers carrying the fetuses inside them and giving birth to calves that they suckle.

A highly social animal, they are known to talk among themselves, sing songs and even imitate human sound. They have a well-earned reputation of being very friendly towards humans with whom they share the propensity to show extreme emotions that include committing suicide!

Whales have been a part of human myth-making since the earliest days. The ancient Greeks, for instance, believed that the Sun God metamorphosed into a dolphin for the express reason of founding his Oracle at Delphi (a holy place of prophesy in those days), on Mount Parnassus. Further according to Greek legends, the dolphins exchanged their life on land for a life in the sea like the fishes, but they did not let go of the righteous spirit they shared with man. This was why killing a dolphin in ancient times was tantamount to killing a man and punishable by death.

The Romans too had some fine legends about the bond between human beings and dolphins and one story in particular, by their philosopher Pliny the elder, about the relationship between a young boy and its dolphin friend is very touching indeed.

However, not all legends associated with whales, particularly the larger species of animals are this benign. The 1851 American novel Moby Dick describes the exploits of an enormous and fearsome white sperm whale that was very ill-disposed towards humans indeed.

Among the most fascinating aspects of the behavior of whales is their tendency to journey vast distances in the great oceans of the world, usually from cold waters where they feed and warm waters where they breed. They may do the travelling alone or in groups, making a grand sight for observers who might watch them from ships or low flying air crafts.

They are so like other land based mammals that they go to sleep as well, but dare not do so for long as they have to periodically surface to breathe. Whales are avid communicators. They do so by executing breath-taking jumps with their vast bodies, flapping their tails on the water's surface and by singing!

Ships are expendable; the whales are not.
-Paul Watson

Why not be like the whale?

When it comes to whales, size does matter and it is not its physical size that we are alluding too. It is the size of their heart, not the physical, but the figurative one. Whales, in spite of being some of the biggest forms of life on earth, (a blue whale is a hundred feet big and almost two hundred tons in weight) are gentle, compassionate and fun-loving animals.

If we can be the same as humans, irrespective of who we are, how important we are and how physically strong, the world would be a better place to live in. Then there is the ability of whales to forge a bond with not just their own species, but with ours as well. There are countless tales of whales coming to the rescue of wrecked ships and drowning sailors. Human beings could learn a lesson or two about empathy from whales and try and understand the perspective of not only one's immediate family, but of whoever one comes in touch with.

The whales are an amazingly playful animal, something which we all know from the antics of dolphins that we witness in giant aquariums or television. However, if one is lucky, one could witness them doing the same on the high seas - indeed a sight for Gods. Over there they jump, and dive and sing to their heart's content. We humans would do well to acquire their *joie de vivre* about life and take each day as it comes and resolve to enjoy it to the fullest.

The epic journeys that the whales undertake every year are worthy of emulation as well. They traverse whole hemispheres in the course of their quest for food and procreation. Couldn't we too aspire to travel to the ends of the world in the quest of what is important to us? What a life that would be?

Lastly, who wouldn't want to be as impossibly powerful as the whales? The largest form of life since life began on earth; the whales have power like no other living thing on earth. The tongue of the blue whale is as heavy as an elephant, and the heart can weigh the same as a car. One can imagine the kind of power such animals can generate. Which human wouldn't like to be enormously powerful physically, even if they can't get as powerful as a whale in a million years?

The Noble Horse

Ever since man got civilized and began to live a somewhat organized and orderly life, the horse has somehow been in the scheme of things, albeit in a round-about way. It primarily became an offensive weapon of war providing mobility to soldiers and letting them march in quest of conquest to the far corners of the globe.

The vast conquests carried out by the Mongols, who at one time lorded over all of Asia and most of Europe, can be directly attributed to their skills as masterly horse riders. Horses, of course, have been used in warfare around the world with ancient Indian, Central Asian, Chinese, Middle Eastern kingdoms deploying them either as cavalry or for drawing war chariots.

When the European powers became ascendant, they too deployed the horses in warfare wherever they went including the Americas. The native American Indians too adopted the horse as a weapon of war and became expert light cavalry troops.

Horses also served to highlight the power and prestige of kings and rulers and continue to do so. Their use on ceremonial occasions includes ceremonial march pasts and the pulling of coaches seating royalty and heads of states.

Till the advent of motor power, horses, and horse-driven vehicles were the fastest way of getting from one place to another. So powerful was the hold of horses on popular imagination that even the capability of motor vehicles was measured in terms of horsepower!

Horses are also an integral part of sports and recreation with equestrian events being quite popular at the Olympics. Polo is a game played on horseback that India gave to the world. Then, of course, there is horse racing which supports a massive betting industry around the world.

Horses are an integral part of the cultural legacy of nations around the world. The various cavalry divisions of armies around the world are still remembered with fond nostalgia. Then there are the famous horses of warrior kings of yore - Bucephalus of Alexander the Great and Chetak of Maharana Pratap back home in India are two examples that immediately come to the mind.

Then there is all the romance associated with the old Wild West in America with cowboys and Red Indians fighting one another on horseback. One of the most alluring cultural images of all time is that of Pegasus the winged horse, which has been used as a logo by a number of corporate brands around the world.

Horses have endeared themselves to mankind for their many sterling qualities. Primary and critical is a horse's self-esteem. This is in evidence when one tries to train a wild horse to do a man's bidding. It will not do so until it is convinced that the potential rider has it in him or her to do so. Otherwise, it will just keep throwing them off.

Strength and stamina too are crucial for a horse. It should be able to carry its rider or pull a cart for long distances at a fairly brisk speed. Courage is another hallmark of horses. They will ride into a battle and sacrifice their lives for their master. They will also lead across pits and jump over fences at their riders' bidding.

Horses can march in perfect unison, pull a carriage in tandem with other horses and even perform circus tricks. Now all of this requires them to be effective learners. They are not just that, but also have distinct personalities of their own, and no two horses will have identical temperaments.

Horses also have a reputation of virility which has been variously represented in popular culture with promiscuous men referred to as studs (the term used to describe a horse that is used for breeding). The sports car Ferrari has a prancing stallion (again a horse kept for breeding) as its logo for the same reason.

In the Chinese zodiac, people born in the year of the horse which falls on 1918, 1930, 1942, 1954, 1966, 1978, 1990, 2002 and 2014 will share certain typical traits. Like the horse, such people will be inclined to be rational, active, optimistic, emotional, and straightforward, which is quite a nice set of traits for any individual to possess.

I call horses 'divine mirrors' - they reflect back the emotions you put in. If you put in love and respect and kindness and curiosity, the horse will return that.
-Allan Hamilton

Horse Sense

In the English language, the idiom horse-sense denotes common sense. The origin of this term probably lies in the American people's love for horses. In any case, the traits of a horse have a lot to do when dealing with practical situations in life where one can get by displaying strength, courage, dexterity, and obedience.

Most people are not rocket scientists and, like the horse would be happy to be both smart and robust enough to be able to face the challenges that come along in life. To be emotional and love one's companions, to have a sense of loyalty to one's group, to be willing to make sacrifices for others; these are the qualities that would serve humans just as well as they serve horses.

Of course, the ladies' men out there would like nothing more than to be referred to as a stud or stallion. Sylvester Stallone was famously nicknamed the *Italian Stallion* in the famous Rocky Movie franchise!

Lion - All Hail the Emperor

There may be animals that are big like the elephant, have the reputation of being the ultimate predator like the tiger or possess the fleet-footedness of the leopard; but there will only be one king of the animal kingdom forever - the lion.

Since the earliest of times, the lion has been identified with regal power across continents and cultures. While the warrior classes of India - the Rajputs and the Sikhs proudly use the surname *Singh*, Sanskrit for lion, the great crusader King Richard of medieval England was renowned as Richard the Lion Heart.

Bravery, in fact, has become synonymous with the lion and being considered *as brave as a lion* is an ultimate compliment for a man. The animal has long been considered the symbol of regal power and we see evidence of this in the four-lion statue emblem known famously as the Lion Capital of Ashoka. This depicted the power of ancient Indian emperor Ashoka and was adopted by modern India as the potent symbol of its statehood.

The lion is also an important symbol for Singapore, the city-state whose name literally means the city of the lion in Sanskrit. The lion head symbol has been adopted by that nation to promote its identity as the Lion City. This is how important the lion is symbolically to nations around the world.

The English have very proudly put its image on several of their coats of arms, even though the animal has nothing whatsoever to do with England!

The ancient Egyptians and Greeks venerated the Sphinx, a creature with the body of a lion and the head of a man. In India, there is the legend of Narasimha, the half lion-half man incarnation of Lord Vishnu. He took on this terrible form to save a devotee Prahlad from certain death at the hands of his father, the demon king Hirnuksahyap.

What is it about lions that spawn tales about their royal or regal ways? Partly it has to do with their being on top of the food chain with no natural enemies in the wild. Being predators, they are admired for their hunting skills as well, but it is in their conduct that one gets glimpses of the origin of their legends.

The lions may be fearsome predators, but they like nothing better than resting and relaxing through the day, sometimes for sixteen to twenty hours. Who but a royal personage could afford such luxury? To relax during the day, and hunt after the sun is down when it's cooler!

Then there is the full-throated roar of the lion, which can be heard an astounding eight kilometers away. They use it to good effect to mark out their territory and let it be known as to whose writ runs there. Is there a more effective way of letting all know that *I am the king around these parts.*

The distinctive mane or the big halo of hair around the head give male lions their uniquely fearsome look. It's almost as if nature has provided them with a crown signifying their royal lineage. Lionesses too display their good breeding in the sense that they are wonderfully caring and loving not just to their own cubs but to that of other lionesses in the pride.

The lions, of course, live as a group in a pride, with a dominant male lion playing the role of the chief, till a younger and stronger male challenges the existing order. How like the kingdoms of the old times!

It's better to be a lion for a day than a sheep all your life.
-Elizabeth Kenny

Be like the lion

With the exception possibly of the tiger, there will not be any animal one would want to be compared with more than the lion - the king himself. So much so that people born under the astrological sun sign Leo or lion consider themselves the salt of the earth, and for good reason.

The Leos carry a regal air around them and like to be the center of attraction. They are proud and vain, yet generous to a fault. While they may exhibit some traits in common with lions, almost anybody would like to possess qualities that typify lions - like strength and power. Who wouldn't like people to defer to them or be in awe of them?

Then there is the legendary bravery of lions. We would all like to be considered lion-hearted - to have the ability to face and surmount any threat or danger. Like lions, we would like to lord it over everyone else. Who wouldn't like their writ to run over all and sundry?

The lion can inspire us to be the first among equals so that our peer group looks up to us. Like the famed loud roar of the lion, our word should command awe and respect among people far and wide. Alexander the Great once declared, "I am not afraid of an army of lions led by a sheep; I am afraid of an army of sheep led by a lion."

It is the ultimate tribute to the lion among people - a person of great heart, courage, and wisdom. It's not even as if it is only the men who can aspire to be like lions. Females can aspire to be like lionesses who take upon themselves the responsibility of hunting for food for their cubs. Aptly in India, a courageous woman is referred to as *Sherni* or lioness.

The male lion performs a stellar role in protecting the members of the pride from any external threat of aggression while the lionesses assign to themselves the role of being nurturers and providers to the young. Together they make for a highly functional family that is able to protect and provide for everyone. This is something that the modern human family, which seems to be falling apart all over the world, can learn a lesson or two from!

Hush...there goes the Wolf.

The relationship between wolves and human beings has been one of intrigue and dark secrets. The wolf straddles the nebulous border between good and evil, righteousness and wickedness in human imagination. That is why the wolf fascinates us. It is an outlaw among animals, at least in our imagination.

All kinds of legends have grown around the supposed supernatural powers of the wolf, especially in the western world. Of these, the legend of the werewolf, sometimes a man and sometimes a wolf is the most widespread. It was believed and one daresay is still believed that a wolf's bite can make a werewolf out of a normal man.

Perfectly normal people are supposed to go crazy and transform into a frenzied wolf baying for anybody's life on a full moon night. This ghastly specter of the werewolf has been a staple fare in countless books, movies and television serials in the western world.

At the same time, there is appreciation for the dark and sinister power of this beast which sends shivers down the spine of its enemies. Perhaps, this was why the famous comic-strip character Phantom, had Devil the wolf as his trusted companion and not a dog.

But not all stories and legends pertaining to wolves are dark. There is one heart-warming Roman legend of the royal twins Romulus and Remus. They were abandoned to die as new born babies by a jealous relative but for the fact that a she-wolf not only rescued them but even suckled the starving babies. They grew up to be the world renowned founders of the mighty city of Rome!

Closer home, we have Kipling's Jungle Book with its story of Mowgli, the orphaned human baby lost on account of his parents' untimely death in the jungles of Central India, being raised by a wolf couple along with their other cubs. Then there is the epic Hollywood movie Dances with Wolves in which the lead character portrayed by Kevin Costner is shown showering love on a wolf in the wilderness, causing the local Indians to name him Dances with Wolves!

A unique love-hate relationship exists between mankind

and the wolves. This could be partly due to the fact that wolves are forebears of our all-time favorite pet the dog, yet retain their wild nature at all times. Unlike a dog, a wolf can't really be domesticated.

Despite their reputation, wolves are a very social animal and live in packs dominated by an alpha male that more often than not has a monogamous relationship with the leading female of the group. Wolves are territorial animals and will mark out their territory and defend it with their all.

They can travel vast distances in search of safe habitat and food. They hunt in packs and whatever food they find, they share among themselves and ensure that the pups are fed as well. The pups are weaned at eight weeks of age after which their disciplining and training for the hunt begins.

I woke up one morning thinking about wolves and realized that wolf packs function as families. Everyone has a role, and if you act within the parameters of your role, the whole pack succeeds, and when that falls apart, so does the pack.
-Jodi Picoult

Wolves and us

In spite of the overall negative image that this magnificent animal has in our consciousness with adages like, *wolf in sheep's clothing* alluding to their alleged negative traits, there is much we can learn from these amazing predators. For starters their family bonds are legendary. The amazing faithfulness that pet dogs exhibit towards their owners is something that can be traced to this trait that they have inherited from their ancestors the wolves - loyalty towards the pack at all costs.

Monogamy is another trait that mankind could learn from these so-called wild animals. For the most part, wolves mate with one partner. What's more, wolves hunt together and provide for the entire pack including the dependent cubs. This again is something that we can look up to these animals for, because unlike us they have to brave tremendous odds and danger to be able to do so. This sometimes involves walking for up to a hundred kilometers.

The wolves start training their cubs very young. They are weaned quite early and put through the drills of hunting to prepare them for life ahead. We modern humans, who tend to make our children soft by providing them with all the manners of luxury, would be better advised to take a leaf out of the wolves' book and prepare our children for the challenges of life a little better.

Loving and caring as they are with their families, they are ferocious hunters and will attack and kill all manner of prey. Yet they will never kill without a reason and are known to be quite shy. This combination of strength and dignity is something we humans could aspire for. Let no one dare trifle with us yet we would not show uncalled for aggression or needlessly boisterous behavior.

Indeed, the wolf is quite a fascinating animal with some very admirable traits that we can emulate.

Clever as the Fox

The fox is our proverbial clever animal. Many of us would have heard the story about the hungry fox that made a vain crow part with the piece of meat in its beak by using the clever stratagem of praising its singing ability. The hapless crow fell for its trick and tried singing in its hideous voice in the process dropping the piece of food right in front of the fox, who, needless to say gobbled it up immediately.

This reputation of the fox, of being a clever or intelligent animal, probably came about by people observing its ways. Being carnivores or meat-eating animals, they have had to devise clever ways of catching their prey. Foxes have the tendency of choosing the easiest and less strenuous way of catching their prey. For instance, foxes thrive quite nicely in the vicinity of towns where there are easy pickings of food.

This often causes conflict with man and in spite of the latter's best efforts to catch these interlopers by laying various kinds of traps; foxes are more often than not able to avoid these. It is possibly this dexterity and cleverness of this animal that led to the English tradition of the Fox Hunt, in which a large number of horsemen and trained dogs take on the poor fox through the wilderness.

In cultures across the world, the fox has been regarded as a wily, clever and even deceitful animal. In medieval England, the famous Norman adventurer was known as Robert the fox, because he was very clever and resourceful.

In oriental legends from China, Korea and Japan foxes are renowned for being mischievous spirits who are not above assuming the form of young human females to seduce men.

The Dogon ethnic group of Africa believes the fox to be a desert god dedicated to the creation of chaos. There is definitely something about the personality of this animal that causes humans to attribute all kinds of trouble to them; so much so that the female of the species is called vixen and we all know how troublesome a human vixen can be!

Genetically related to dogs and wolves, the fox shares their trait of loyalty, but are far too shy for one to fully appreciate that. Not being able to use sheer ferociousness like its other canine cousins, it is, however, able to use its cleverly wired brain to make the best of the resources available to it.

Though they will not eat about anything, they do like to

search far and wide in search of food and are known to often explore all kinds of inaccessible places in that quest. Never ones to show off like a dog might, they are however in quite good physical shape, by virtue of their robust lifestyle.

The mystique of the foxes also arises from the fact that they are partly nocturnal animals and one can imagine the impact on seeing a fox with its bushy tail slither away into the forest in the silvery moonlight!

With foxes we must play the fox.
-Thomas Fuller

The fox and us

Now what is it that a fox can teach us, some might say? Plenty if one realizes that like the fox, we are not always the strongest and it is our clever-thinking and optimal usage of the resources that are available to us that make us get ahead in life. And what is wrong in being clever and wily?

Isn't man so much like the fox - not the most powerful of people but with his smart brain, manages to outfox every other species. There, now you know the origin of the word outfox! So really, to be like a fox is to be like your own self. We are essentially similar creatures - clever, inquisitive, and adventurous and always allowing discretion to be the better part of valor.

One can learn from the fox to be clever yet not pretentious, wily but capable of showing loyalty where needed and lastly extremely capable yet shy and oblivious of one's superlative reputation. The more you think of it, the more relatable the traits of a fox appear.

A fox-like person is sure to be very successful in his career for his personality would be quite at home in the competitive and often treacherous environment that unfortunately pervades in such a set up. A no-nonsense person, who is always thinking of the best way to get the job done without a minimum of fuss would have an advantage over a flamboyant braggart who would invariably blow his chances.

One can imagine people with fox-like personality doing very well for themselves as lawyers, marketing managers, brokers and even detectives. Remember that old German detective serial Old Fox, the English dubbed version of which was such a rage on Indian television many years ago.

Gentle as a Deer

Nothing epitomizes the peaceful idyllic of a place in time than the sight of a deer gamboling about or having a drink at a poolside somewhere. A deer is an animal that fearsome predators love preying on, and it is this vulnerability combined with the deer's amazing beauty and grace that makes it stand out in our imagination as a symbol of all that is good and noble.

Deer are, of course, forever imprinted in the consciousness of all Hindus, as being the animal that led to the travails of Lord

Rama and his wife Sita. The latter chanced upon a beautiful golden deer while in exile in the forests along with her husband. So enchanted was she by the beauty of the animal that she sent him on a disastrous errand to capture that beautiful animal and bring it to her.

Unknown to both of them, the beautiful deer was, in reality, a demon, who had assumed that shape on the orders of his master the demon King Ravana. With Rama away, looking for the enchanting deer in the far reaches of the forest, Ravana swooped down in his royal aircraft and managed to abduct the unguarded Sita, thereby setting the stage for an epic battle between the forces of righteousness represented by Lord Rama and that of evil represented by Ravana.

In ancient Egypt, the Goddess of hunt Satet, had the horns of a deer and sometimes its face as well. The Scythian people of Eurasia and Central Asia believed the stag (male deer) to be sacred and its motifs can often be found among their artwork. In the Shinto religion of Japan, deer are supposed to be messengers to the gods.

Deer are found in all the continents save Australia and Antarctica. There are about a hundred types of this animal that inhabit different parts of the world. These animals are blessed with some wonderful faculties that enable them to do quite well for themselves in the various kinds of environment that they are placed in. These include an incredible ability to hear, which is much superior to that of humans. That apart, they can run at a blistering forty miles per hour and jump as high as 10 feet. Besides, they are excellent swimmers and their strong sense of smell warns them of the presence of predators from a long distance away.

When faced with danger the deer takes to its heels with graceful alacrity. Its nimbleness and fleet-footedness save the day most of the time as this feisty animal more often than not successfully outruns powerful predators many times its size. Its diet largely comprises of green plants, nuts, shoots, leaves and grasses. It, therefore, has almost no excess fat. This enables it to display amazing athleticism in its movements on account of its lean and well-honed muscles.

Deer are, in fact, remarkably adaptable animals as their geographic spread would show. They like living in areas between the edge of the forest and the contiguous crop lands enabling them to graze in the open and shelter in the woods.

I ask people why they have deer heads on their walls. They always say because it's such a beautiful animal. There you go. I think my mother is attractive, but I have photographs of her."
— Ellen DeGeneres

Be a deer, dear

What is it that we can learn from this hoofed animal? Above everything else, we can learn to be a peaceable creature like the deer. It threatens no one and wants nothing more than to be left to its own devices. We can endeavor to be the kind of person whose very presence spreads a sense of peace and calm.

It would be great for humans to possess the ability of not only creating a peaceful environment around us but when faced with a crisis, have the ability to use every muscle and sinew in our body to achieve safety. We can aspire to the amazingly graceful athleticism of the deer - perhaps we need to visit the gym more often for that!

If in spite of its gentle nature the deer can on occasions run at speeds of 40 miles an hour and jump ten feet; it has got to have the heart of a champion to achieve it! Now that is something any human being worth his or her salt would like to possess.

The versatility of a deer as a species enables it to survive in all kinds of environments - from the reindeer of the Arctic region to the cheetal deer of the tropical forests in India and from thick woods to marshy grasslands the deer is a hardy animal that is able to thrive anywhere if left undisturbed.

We could do well to be similarly versatile in our own lives. That would enable us to adjust to varying environments with ease and allow us to excel unimpeded by factors like geography and climate. In fact, the very fact that mankind is known to do quite well for itself in every nook and corner of the globe and even in space shows that we have something of the deer in us!

Beware the Shark

Nothing strikes more primeval terror in the hearts of human beings than the prospect of a shark attack. The role of the great Hollywood blockbuster Jaws in demonizing this large but shy (hard to believe, but true!) fish from the deep seas can't be underestimated. The reality is that most sharks avoid humans and are known to shun contact. They definitely have been victims of very bad prcss!

It's not as if sharks don't attack human beings. They do occasionally, and the most dramatic instance of this was the recent televised attack upon three time world champion surfer Mike Fanning at the South African J Bay Open championship. But such instances are very, very rare indeed (6 times in a year!), and on the whole, sharks offer a negligible threat to humans swimming out there in the seas.

But one can trust human beings to push the envelope and swim next to sharks undersea, but within the safety of an iron cage is an idiosyncratic example of this. Now who is invading whose space? Sharks attacking human beings in what is essentially their habitat is akin to us attacking a snake or a rodent who happens to sneak into our home.

However, not all humans revile the sharks. In fact in Hawaiian legend and folklore, there are a number of shark gods! There are similar legends and myths to be found among Australian aboriginals, North American Indians and several tribes from the Indonesian region. In modern times, however, it is their image as a dangerous and carnivorous predator that naturally comes to mind when you think about sharks.

One might even say that the image is right in the sense that sharks are voracious meat eaters. But they certainly don't feed on humans. Their diet primarily comprises of a variety of creatures like sea turtles, seals, fish, octopi, lobsters, squids and other species of sharks!

Part of the reason why sharks inspire such terror is their perceived large size. It is true that some sharks are really large, like the whale shark (up to 60 feet) or the much feared great white shark (23 feet) which is the main protagonist in the movie, Jaws and was the one identified as being responsible for the attack on Mike Fanning.

However, there are also sharks the size of one's hand; so to base one's fear of this animal merely on its presumed large size is misplaced. However, the importance of sharks as part of the ocean's eco-system is indubitable. These fearsome predators are on top of the food chain that keep the number of other marine species in check. Any fall in the shark numbers can have disastrous consequences for the fragile marine ecology.

Sharks are peerless hunters, who have perfected the art of hunting prey. Their sense of smell, hearing, sight, touch and taste is extraordinary giving them an unsurpassed advantage over the animals they prey upon. Add to this their ability to detect the presence of prey by reading electric signals emanating from them, and you have a predator extraordinaire.

As if this wasn't enough, their sleek torpedo-shaped bodies that literally glide through water like greased lightening help them outwit and outsmart the intended victim with consummate ease. Is it any wonder that the shark inspires such awe amongst both its prey and its awe-struck land based observers - us?

Sharks are beautiful animals, and if you're lucky enough to see lots of them that means that you're in a healthy ocean. You should be afraid if you are in the ocean and don't see sharks.
-Sylvia Earle

Animal to emulate

Humans love to be compared with sharks. Ask Greg Norman, the great PGA golfing champion, why he is called the Great

White Shark, and you might get a wide smile as a reply. It is their skill as hunters and the precision with which they go for their kill, which probably makes sports champions take to sharks. However, the dogged tenacity with which sharks get their victims is possibly also the reason why usurious money lenders are referred to as loan sharks! They will get their money back from the hapless loaner come what may.

The sheer brooding physicality of the shark and the danger associated with them is what probably attracts the males of the human species to this animal. This element of intensity and mystery backed by extraordinary physical prowess appeals to the hunter instinct that human males carry in their DNA.

It is a fact that their physical features and abilities approach perfection in what they are programmed to achieve - hunting for food. They have been doing it for far longer than mankind's time on earth, for the sharks have been around longer than dinosaurs, and have had millions of years to practice.

If one were to emulate their single-minded dedication towards the hunt and relentlessly pursue our goals with the primeval dedication of a shark, nothing will be able to stop us from achieving the goals. The early cultures of mankind who were far more in touch with nature than modern humans revered the shark for a reason. They instinctively knew that there was much to be learnt from these creatures who are our elders in chronological terms.

It is time that mankind showed these much-maligned creatures the respect that is due to them. After all, they are the great survivors and it is something that we would like to be as well!

Soar like the Eagle.

The eagle is a stately bird, make no mistake about it. This large and powerful bird of prey with its characteristic hooked beak, wide-span of wings, fantastic eyesight and the ability to soar high in the air is in a unique class of its own.

Add to it their power, awesome hunting skills, and apparently regal bearing; the eagle presents a very stately image of itself indeed. Is it any surprise that it can be found on more coats of arms representing nations, royal kingdoms and religious orders than any other bird and animal?

No surprise, therefore that the massive Bald Eagle with its eight-foot wing span is the national symbol of the mightiest country in the world, the United States. There is something very impressive about the very sight of the eagle for mankind to want to appropriate it as a symbol of all that is stately, noble and grand.

The ancient Celts used to believe that eagles were the wisest of all creatures, save the salmon. In Wales where the Golden Eagles were once found, the cry of an eagle was supposed to herald a positive event like the birth of a child. Interestingly, eagle feathers are considered special both by Scottish highland clan chiefs who wear them in their hats and Native Americans who wear them in their headdresses.

There are more than sixty types of eagles to be found around the world. Some varieties like the Harpy Eagle and Philippine Eagle are even able to carry off large prey such as deer and monkey, making these magnificent birds the truly fearsome predators they are reputed to be. What adds to their fearsomeness is the fact that their eyesight is so good that some eagles can spot a rabbit from a distance of two miles!

Not only are these birds fierce predators, they are quite intelligent as well. They are known to drop turtles from a great height onto the rocks below to crack open the shells and get to the meat! Their unique ability to fly high and glide gracefully in the air for long periods of time has long awed people. Not only can they do that, but they can also execute a sudden dive to attack a prey or retrieve a falling piece of meat.

An eagle is also looked upon as a symbol of unbridled freedom and power. No wonder these birds were revered by many cultures so much so that the Aztecs would build a city on a spot where an eagle had landed! Their high flying abilities made some religions believe that they had the ability to touch the face of God.

Eagles don't flock, you have to find them one at a time.
-Ross Perot

Being like the eagle

Man has long wanted to be regal and stately like the eagle. That is why it is used so often as a state symbol. As the eagle symbolizes all that is exalted, being like the eagle means that one is a free spirit who brooks no interference. Like the eagle, one exudes power and like it, one would like to soar high above everybody else.

So to be like the eagle is not only to be noble but also very ambitious. Like the eagle, such people also possess the power and skills to realize one's goals. An eagle-like person would be relentless in overcoming any obstacles or hindrances in one's path.

You will not find eagles forming flocks as they don't need the safety of numbers to protect themselves. They are on top of the food chain and masters of all that they survey. An eagle-type of person will likewise have the wherewithal to take his own decisions and stand by them. There is no looking over their shoulder or seeking reassurance from others for such people. They would most likely be leaders that others would gladly emulate.

Blessed with extraordinary vision, an eagle can plan and execute a hunt with exact precision. An eagle-like person would be able to use its superior foresight and vision to plan ahead meticulously and fully obtain the objectives.

Then there is the courage and determination of eagles which makes them attack large animals like goats and monkey and prevail over them. We too could emulate them and fearlessly meet the stiffest of challenges by learning to punch much above our weights.

It's not for nothing that the eagle is universally admired and looked up to. We would be well-advised to be like the eagle and soar way above our contemporaries and peers. To be like the eagle is to have your head up in the clouds; not in pride and arrogance, but secure in the knowledge that one's lofty position is unassailable and permanent.

No wonder many empires of old like the Indian Vijayanagar Empire, the Ottoman Empire of the Turks, the Roman Empire, and the Persian Empire had the symbol of the eagle represent their glory. To be like the eagle is to be imperial and impervious; much exalted above everyone else.

As pretty as a Flamingo

A flock of pink flamingos flying overhead or just standing in shallow marshes is a sight to behold. As they do most of their flying at night, one can consider oneself lucky if one has indeed seen them do that. Seeing them wade or stand in water in their hundreds is a mesmerizing sight as their pink color makes them so conspicuous.

Also, their peculiar habit of standing on one leg and folding up the other one is something that not just presents a unique picture but has also perplexed scientists about why they do so.

Some of them conjecture that they do this to preserve their body heat standing in cold frigid waters. But then they are known to do that in tropical regions as well, where the waters are anything but cold!

Other scientists think that standing on one leg makes them take to the air faster, in case of a predator attack, while there are those who attribute the trait to their need to rest a leg! In any case, their standing on one leg combined with their bright coloring and long and graceful careening neck certainly make them look iconic - some would even say celestial.

It is almost inevitable that a bird as large and pretty as the flamingo would have been considered holy at some point in human history. To the ancient Egyptians, flamingos represented the God Ra on earth. The Moche people of Peru venerated the flamingos as well and often represented them in their art. The flamingo enjoys the status of the national bird in The Bahamas.

The flamingos that can grow up to be almost five feet tall are omnivorous creatures and feed on a varied diet that comprises of insects, larvae, algae, snails, fish, lobsters, shrimps, and crabs. They are an extremely social creature and have to be at least ten in number if one hopes to keep them alive in captivity.

Their gregarious nature and tendency to stick together in flocks or colonies enables them to protect their numbers from predators. The adults, in fact, make a conscious effort to protect the young amongst them. Another striking feature about flamingos is that they are monogamous and will mate with one partner throughout their lives.

Flamingos enjoy a fairly long life span and there has been

an instance of a flamingo living to an age of 83 in captivity! They are in fact a thriving species of birds with millions of their numbers to be found all over the world. Colonies of flamingos can often have thousands of members and there is famously even a one million flamingo strong colony to be found in East Africa!

Stay happy like the flamingo

The flamingo is a gregarious, social, happy and long-lived bird. It eats almost anything, has a fabulous social circle and is a faithful mate. Is it any surprise that they are found in such large numbers and live a long fulfilling life?

That apart, they are pretty and eccentric as well! Every single trait of the flamingo would stand a human being in good stead. Who would say no to a lifetime of being with lots of friends, socializing all the time, eating a wide variety of cuisines and having the love of your mate for a lifetime? Add to that good looks and a uniquely attractive body posture and your happiness would be complete.

But there is more, your species would never be threatened and you would get to live to a ripe old age. What more would a man or a woman aspire to be?

The success of the flamingo as a species is on account of their lifestyle choices. They live together in large numbers, eat a varied and balanced diet and spend most of their time out in the open on the water's edge. By keeping things simple, they have made it easy for their species to do extremely well for themselves.

We could ourselves try to make lifestyle changes where we pay more attention to our social life; the way we eat, and how well-bonded we are with our life partner. That apart, time spent away from the urban sprawl and closer to nature would help us heal ourselves mentally, physically and spiritually. We would then be in the pink of health - a flamingo pink!

A Leopard

The leopard is the lesser known and less glamorous member of the large cat family but is every bit as powerful and ferocious. What's more, the leopard is a wily survivor and is found in much larger numbers than either the more famous tiger or lion. If you harbored the illusion that leopards couldn't hold a candle when it came to inspiring terror in the hearts of man, think again. Jim Corbett the famous writer, hunter and conservationist regarded this animal every bit as dangerous and wily as the tiger. His book, The Man-eating Leopard of Rudraprayag is a testimony to this.

The hold of the leopard on human imagination is immense and there are numerous legends associated with the leopard that abound in much of Africa, the Middle East, and Central Asia. It is not, therefore, surprising to find this magnificent animal represented in much of their mythology and artwork.

The leopard is also well-represented in the old European tradition. The ancient Greeks believed that it was the preferred mount of the God Dionysus. In ancient Egypt, priests wore leopard skin. In China, the figure of the leopard was embroidered on the robes of generals in the hope that they would obtain some of the animal's strength and ferocity.

The leopard's success as a species is attributable to a number of reasons. These include its smarter hunting tactics, the fact that its fur lends to a very effective camouflage and its tree climbing ability. Add to this the fact that it has the strength and the tendency to carry away heavy prey. It has the further ability of being able to hide the carcass in the branches of trees.

Its great strength comes from its varied diet that includes dung beetles, a variety of primates, deer, antelope and even rodents and birds.

It is a hardy and adaptable animal that can be found in a variety of terrains like rain forests, grasslands, and mountainous regions. One can easily recognize the leopard by its yellow coat that carries the distinctive black spots. Though these animals are smaller than other large cats, they are stronger by weight and have the ability to even take on prey that is relatively big in size.

They are quite agile and can work up to speeds in excess of 58 kilometers an hour. Besides they can manage to leap up to twenty feet horizontally and manage a vertical jump of almost ten feet. By nature, they are quite shy and elusive and move about mainly at night. Left to themselves they would avoid human contact.

Stealthy as a leopard

A leopard-like person would be a master strategist. They would use stealth, guile, and strength in just the right measure to achieve their objective. Such a person would be a great survivor and their adaptability and dexterity would make them face both adversity and good times with equanimity.

A great person to have around in times of a crisis, a leopard-like person despite its obvious strength would not be very overt about what they can achieve. There would be an element of the mysterious and the unknown about such a person.

A leopard though smaller than a lion or a tiger is known to frighten even elephants when it is enraged and ready to charge. Similarly, a leopard-like man would make an extremely dangerous enemy and people would be well-advised not to cross swords with such a person.

Leopards are known to be able to become one with their environment in that the color of their coat and the shape of their spots undergo a subtle change that suits the surrounding topography. People who are able to make themselves comfortable irrespective of where they are will have an advantage over those who are more rigid and fixed in their ways.

The former will find more success in life than the latter;

much in the way that leopards are on the whole doing better than the other large cats. People in professions like marketing, law and share broking can be said to possess leopard-like abilities in that they constantly evolve their strategies. Like the leopard, they may not enjoy an extraordinary reputation in the popularity sweepstakes, but when it comes to meeting their objectives, they will do so with unerring efficiency.

The Serpent

The serpent or the snake does not have a very wholesome reputation. This is largely on account of it being represented as an agent of the devil in The Bible. The serpent enticed Eve to eat the forbidden apple, who in turn caused Adam to do the same, leading to their banishment from the paradise.

The implausibility of this scenario notwithstanding, it did sow the seed of an at times irrational fear of snakes among people. It's not as if snakes cannot be dangerous. There are fatalities caused by snake-bite, but these are more often than not because of fear, rather than the venom in the bite.

The fact of the matter is that a negligible percentage of snakes are poisonous, and of the ones that are, again a very small percentage carry enough venom or poison to be able to kill a human being. On the contrary, snakes are enormously helpful to humans, as they feed on rodents and other pests that would otherwise wreak terrible damage on our food crops.

As is usually the case, the snakes have a much better reputation in the East. In India, for example, the prime Gods Shiva and Vishnu are closely associated with serpents. The former wears a cobra around his neck while the latter rests on the coils of a massive multi-headed snake. Then there are the legendary Naga people who are shape shifters, alternating between human and snake manifestations. As honorable people they wreak terrible vengeance on those humans who wrong them.

Not ones to show a similar nuanced approach to all of God's creatures, the latest from the stable of western literature, the famed Harry Potter series again depicts the serpent as an accomplice of the arch villain, Voldemort.

The Chinese, on the other hand, show far more respect for this much misunderstood and reviled animal. The snake is one of the prominent sun signs of their zodiac. People born under this sign are supposed to be very wise and wily on account of their lives' experiences, and it is well-nigh impossible for them to be deceived.

What are the snakes really like? Most of them, as we are aware of, don't have any limbs and move by slithering about. They have good vision but cannot hear and depend upon sensing the vibrations emanating from the ground with their bodies. Though they don't have any vocal chords, they are able to produce a hissing sound.

Snakes feed on insects and small animals and do not pose a danger or threat to humans, except when they feel threatened themselves. Not only do they keep a check on the numbers of destructive (from a human point of view) animals, their venom is harvested to be used to treat certain diseases and also to make antivenin to treat snake-bite.

Beside, snakes are eaten by some East Asian countries, and their skin, of course, is much prized in the fashion industry where it is used to make belts, bags, shoes and purses.

Even if a snake is not poisonous, it should pretend to be venomous.
-Chanakya

Me? A snake?

That would likely be the reaction if one were to be compared to a serpent. There is so much prejudice against this animal; that being called a serpent is anything but a compliment. But there are those who like the dark and sinister connotations that a mention of the snake brings to the mind.

That is why many of the criminal gangs in our movies and crime thriller fiction are named the Cobra. The Cobra is also a popular brand of beer! So the snakes do have something going for them. Amongst Hindus snakes are also referred to as *nagas*, a term which is most certainly not pejorative. In fact, snakes are worshiped on the day of the Nagapanchami festival, harking back to the theme that religions of the East show a lot of reverence to nature and all that constitutes it.

So in the Indian context, being compared to a naga may not

be considered offensive at all. In fact, such a person is looked upon as a protector, who would guard you the same way as the nagas are the traditional custodians of treasure in Hindu mythology. Even if you look at the story from The Bible, the snake encouraged Eve and Adam to eat the apple from the tree of knowledge, so that they became aware of the fact that they were roaming around like naked savages! God wanted to keep Adam and Eve in the perpetual bliss of ignorance.

So what is it about the snake that is not to be liked? It rids us of pests who would do harm, provides its venom to be used as medicine, and its skin to be fashioned into fashion accessories. So if like a snake one rids the society of evil, helps cure sick people and is useful in some way or the other even after death, isn't one a cut above everybody else?

Proud as a Peacock

The peacock is quite simply the most beautiful creation of the animal kingdom. When it chooses to dazzle us with a full display of its brilliantly colored feathers, we are left mesmerized. So it was fair to assume that the peacock must be a proud bird, hence the expression, *Proud as a Peacock.*

If indeed it was proud, perhaps it had the right to be, as no less a being than Lord Krishna himself would wear a peacock feather in his headgear! Found abundantly in India the peacock is the country's national bird. Amongst the most popular motifs in Indian artworks till date, it can be found extensively on murals, paintings, and even textiles.

The ancient Greeks revered the peacock as they believed that the bird was associated with Hera, the queen of the gods. In the 14th century Europe, peacocks were considered prized pets by the rich and the powerful. This association with wealth and splendor saw the Moghul Emperor Shah Jahan order the making of the grand Peacock Throne, the one that Persian conqueror Nadir Shah carted away to Iran after his famous sacking of Delhi in 1739. Perhaps he was inspired by the reverence with which the peacock has always been regarded in ancient Persia, to bring to his country, albeit as a looted trophy, the most famous peacock themed artifact of all time!

The Christians regard the peacock to be a holy symbol as well, as it is supposed to represent the church. For the Hindus, the peacock is to be revered because it is the symbol of Lakshmi the Goddess of wealth. Wealth and splendor seem to be somehow inextricably associated with the peacock. The peacock is also the mount of the God of war Kartikeya.

The piéce de résistance in so far as peacocks' claim to fame is concerned is their magnificent plumage, which adorns the body of the male peacock, it is conjectured to attract the opposite sex. Like with humans, it is the showman who gets the gals!

Unlike its somewhat aristocratic image, a peacock is an omnivore and in the wild feeds on a varied diet that can comprise of plants, grass, seeds, flower petals, insects, small mammals and even snakes!

Oh to be like the peacock

No one would mind being compared to the peacock - a symbol of beauty, riches and divinity! At the same time it would perhaps be good to ape the bird in its practical approach towards food, its splendid plumage notwithstanding.

Like in the case of a peacock, one's life should be a celebration of beauty and its accompanying positivity. The riches and regal splendor associated with this bird too are something that any man or woman, would welcome in their lives. The fact that it also is associated with God and spirituality means that one can aspire to be both wealthy and spiritual in life.

All this really points to a life full of happiness and fulfillment. So really, to be like a peacock is to be one extremely happy and fulfilled person. The peacock, therefore, can inspire anyone to make their lives more vibrant, meaningful and ultimately happy. Man does not live by bread alone. There is a higher calling in life and the peacock symbolizes it.

To be like the Swan

The swan is an achingly beautiful bird. Is it any surprise to discover that it features prominently in art and literature? The word 'swan' itself is one of the oldest in the English language and it certainly vests this stately white colored water bird with a hoary tradition that goes back to the mists of antiquity.

The proverbial swan song has its origins in ancient Greece. It was believed that swans sang the most beautiful songs of their lives just before they died. Then there is the old legend of the swan maidens who have the ability to change from a human shape into one of swan's. The famous ballet The Swan Lake is also premised on this legend.

The Greeks believed that the God Zeus assumed the shape of a swan to be with Leda, a mortal woman he loved. The Celtic

Goddess Brighid too is associated with swans. In the cold parts of the world that have bleak and snowy winters, the swan is considered a harbinger of spring in that it is amongst the first creatures to start swimming around in the various water bodies once winter has receded.

As a species, swans are close cousins of ducks and geese. Their most remarkable trait is that they mate for life. Another noteworthy trait is the ferocious manner in which they protect the nests. In fact, one man lost his life due to drowning in one such ferocious defense.

Swans are primarily herbivores with their diet comprising mainly of roots, tubers, stems, leaves and the like, both on land and in water. They will sometimes eat frogs, fish, and worms as well.

Among the Hindus, the swan known as the Hamsa, is revered as the mount of Saraswati the Goddess of learning. A swan-like person is a much-exalted human being according to Hindu tenets as they are not overly attached to the world despite being a part of it, just like a swan though in the water, does not get its feathers wet. As a matter of fact, the Sanskrit term *Paramhansa* is an honorific for a person who has attained great spiritual learning.

Swan like personage

As described above, the Hindus consider it to be a great honor to be compared to a swan, as it is supposed to denote spiritual achievement. There are other attributes of the swan which human beings would do well to emulate.

Its love for its mate and the sense of fidelity is something that we could imbibe. Then there is the dedication with which swans will protect their nests. Perhaps we could learn a thing or two from them. Protecting one's home and hearth with extreme ferociousness is a trait any human would identify with completely.

Just like the very sight of swans swimming about placidly in lakes, ponds, and other water bodies signals the approach of spring in countries with cold climates, a swan-like countenance in a human being could dispel gloom wherever such a person sets foot. So if you are the person whose mere presence lights up the atmosphere and brightens the mood of everyone around, then you indeed are blessed with a swan-like countenance.

The swan, despite its exquisite looks, is quite a practical eater displaying its pragmatism when it comes to matters of survival. Similarly, we could adopt a similarly flexible and accommodating approach in the way we live our lives no matter how exalted and superior to others we might imagine that we are.

Swan is beauty and grace personified. That is why it has inspired art and literature since the earliest times - not just in the West but in India as well. Here it is a metaphor for not only outer beauty but inner beauty as well. Humans would do well to aspire to be like the swans, as beautiful on the outside as on the inside.

The Grace of a Giraffe

If there is an animal that epitomizes grace it has to be the giraffe. Tall, statuesque, yet so delicate in the way that it conveys itself. The fact that it is the tallest living terrestrial animal with a uniquely patterned coat and an extremely long neck make it appear very striking. One will often find children making a beeline to the giraffe enclosure at any zoo.

It is but natural to find many myths and legends associated with this animal in its homeland. In South Africa, the giraffe dance is performed to treat ailments of the head. Of course, its tremendous height is the source of a number of legends explaining it. In East African legends, it is attributed to the eating of a lot of magic herbs!

Their 9 to 15-foot frame which weighs between 0.6 to 1.9 tonnes is entirely supported by feeding on leaves from the top of acacia and Commiphora leaves. Their size makes most giraffes safe from predator attacks, but younger giraffes do fall prey to lions, leopards, hyenas and African wild dogs.

For its huge size giraffes can work up to quite a speed with its running and are known to hit sixty kilometers an hour. Incredibly a giraffe needs to sleep only between ten minutes and two hours in a 24 hour period - the shortest sleep requirement of any mammal! Stooping down to drink makes giraffes very vulnerable, but fortunately, they don't have to do that very often, as they obtain most of their water requirement from leaves!

Giraffes have double the blood pressure of humans because their blood needs to be pumped up all the way to its head. Its great height comes to the fore in everything associated with it. Female giraffes give birth to their offspring standing, which causes the newborns to drop five feet! It takes the newborns just half an hour to be standing on their feet.

Their great height notwithstanding, giraffes are quite a social lot and generally go about their lives peacefully. Once in a while, they show aggression by swinging their necks, but that usually doesn't harm anyone. Their pleasant demeanor led people in the old days to make presents of this animal to the royalty!

While giraffes are known to be gentle and peaceable, they can fight too. In fact, they can kick so hard that they are known to kill lions and crocodiles by the sheer force of their assault.

So it is not as if giraffes are any kind of pushovers, just because they have a peaceful nature!

Giraffes are completely tranquil - they have no predators as adults because there's not an animal in the jungle stupid enough to go for them.

 - Joanna Lumley

Learn from the giraffe

For an animal the size of the giraffe, one would imagine that it would be an ungainly presence; but one look at the grace with which it moves its long body will dispel the notion. The way they gallop across open grasslands presents an achingly beautiful sight.

For humans, they present a valuable lesson on how to conduct oneself with grace and not be constrained by the way one is physically. They also teach that to be big does not have to mean overbearing. One can be a giant and yet be gentle.

From the baby giraffes, we can learn what it means to hit the deck running. They are on their feet half an hour after birth and running around with their mother in a few hours. We humans take an awfully long time to grow up and be responsible for ourselves!

The simplicity of diet is another thing that we can pick up from giraffes. They merely feed on some leaves for their sustenance. Like the giraffe, we can be peaceful yet capable of facing the mightiest of threats, when the need arises. The giraffe that eats some leaves can kill a lion with a mere kick!

Let us have that kind of quiet confidence about our abilities and what we can do, and the world can be ours!

Look at the Rhinoceros

If ever there were an animal built like a battle tank, it is the rhinoceros or rhino. The reason for its rather strange looks is the fact that it is a primitive form of mammal that traces its origin to the millions of years old Miocene era.

As many are aware rhinos are of two main types - the two-horned African variety and the single horn Indian one. Its horn is supposed to contain aphrodisiacal and other medicinal properties and for this reason, the poor animal has been almost hunted to extinction.

Apart from humans, the rhino faces no danger from any kind of predators as its thick hide (1.5 to 5cm) and massive frame (more than 2000kg weight) completely insulates it from attack. Like other giants of the animal kingdom, the elephant, and the giraffe, the rhino is a vegetarian surviving on leafy material, trees, shrubs and grass.

They are known to be short-tempered and are often seen charging with their head lowered when agitated. They can run quite fast, genetically related as they are to horses and zebras! However, for the most part, they are quite sorted and like nothing more than grazing peacefully on a grassland, preferably next to a water hole.

Their eyesight is poor, but this is compensated by an excellent sense of smell and hearing. Rhinos make very good mothers, forging a close bond with their calves for as much as two to four years.

Among the famous legends associated with the rhino is the one created by Kipling about how a rhino came about its peculiar skin. The thick skin is attributed to the punishment it received for stealing a Parsee's cake. Among the tenets of Buddhism is the Rhinoceros sutra, which enjoins man to give up worldly pleasures and take to solitary contemplation, much in the fashion of a solitary rhinoceros roaming the forests by itself.

A peculiar trait shared by both the African and Indian rhinos is the symbiotic relationship they share with certain species of birds. The birds feed on the ticks and other insects on the animal's back and also create a commotion if they sense danger.

Not only do the Chinese have a yen for using powdered rhino horn in many of their traditional medicines, other Asian nations too imagine it to provide the cure for a multitude of diseases including asthma, dog bites, epilepsy, snake bite, dysentery and everything else you can think of. No wonder the poachers have almost decimated the species.

The children danced on. They were alive; that is all that mattered. They lived for the moment. They danced when they could, and died when they would."
— Lawrence Anthony, *The Last Rhinos: My Battle to Save One of the World's Greatest Creatures*

Like a rhino

What do we learn from a species that has almost been wiped out by human greed? Not to be greedy and superstitious; to respect all of God's creatures and allow them to live with dignity. We may consider this animal primitive, but it does not prey on others, and certainly does not indulge in senseless slaughter.

On the contrary it lets birds; members of another species to feed off the insects on its body. It's a mutually beneficial relationship of course, but for that, you need to be able to peacefully coexist.

We can also learn to be as tough as the rhino. A fully grown rhino fears no predators. If we could learn to be just as fearless and not be cowed down into submission by anyone we would be able to live truly gloriously indeed.

Then there is the wonderful bond a rhino mother has with its cub, never leaving its side and protecting it from all kinds of danger. Perhaps a human mother could learn a thing or two from this very primitive mammal.

A rhino is intimately associated with Mother Nature with its feet firmly planted on earth. It lives in complete harmony with nature. We as humans have moved away from nature with disastrous consequences like global warming staring us in the face. We need to shed our ego and cruelty towards our fellow living beings.

Instead of slaughtering rhinos we should instead be like them and intimately link ourselves to Mother Nature.

Clever Crow

The crow may not be much to look at, but it is one clever bird. We are all aware of that story about the thirsty crow from the Indian classic *Panchatantra Tales*. This is the one where the crow throws pebbles into a pitcher of water to raise the level of the liquid high enough for him to drink it with its beak.

It so happens that science agrees with the contention being made in this tale. The crows are indeed a very intelligent species of birds. According to a study, their intelligence matches that of a seven-year-old human child. As a matter of fact, they are the only non-primate species that makes and uses tools!

For all its positives, the crow has sometimes been depicted negatively in popular culture, probably because of its dark color. There are old legends in the Scotland which talk of people turning into a crow because of a curse. Among the American Indian tribes, though, crows are thought to be harbingers of good fortune. The Hindus generally regard the crow as a bad omen, and calling someone a crow is quite an insult!

In medieval times, some people believed that crows could prophesize the future including the possibility of rain or even a battle! Many indeed are the myths and legends associated with these birds.

Crows occur in large groups oddly called murder and these could number from hundreds to thousands. They are a very playful species and one can hear of many instances of their naughty playfulness. This includes imitating the sounds made by other birds! Somehow playfulness and naughtiness seem to be essential ingredients of behavior displayed by intelligent species.

Crows are omnivorous and feed on a variety of food that encompasses fruits, nuts, earthworms, seeds, eggs, and carrion. They live a reasonably long life that can stretch to twenty years. There is even a documented case of one crow having lived to be 59!

So remarkable is this bird that different groups or *murders* develop their own dialects for communicating among themselves. They have an uncanny ability to remember faces, and if one has had the bad fortune of offending them, they will not only make a concerted attack, but also remember the face of the offender, and spread the word not just to others in the group, but to the coming generations as well.

Crows are incredibly smart. They can be taught five things on the drop.

-Robbie Coltrane

What do we learn from the crows?

Being industrious and sharp-witted top the list. In spite of the fact that the crow is a mere bird, it is actually able to fashion tools and use them. How much better can we, who are so much better endowed than them, perform if we would leverage our faculties to the fullest?

The social cohesion that crows show is inspirational. They will come to the rescue of any of their member who is in distress. This is something that the so-called superior beings humans lack so much. We are all essentially so self-centered. It's each for himself.

By watching out for each other, the crows are able to protect their own from harm. Their terrific memory that imprints the face of an offender in their collective memory and that too for posterity is an awesome ability to possess - something that we humans could definitely use.

The joie de vivre that crows exhibit is again something that humans could adopt. Being naughty and playful seems to keep these creatures in fine fettle and probably keeps their mental abilities ship-shape. Perhaps we too should take life less seriously and look at the brighter side of things. Who knows, it might even make us smarter.

Their varied diet points to the fact that they are practical creatures and know what is good for their survival. Humans too could be less rigid and more willing to move out of their comfort zone in order to not just survive, but also thrive.

Truly the crow could teach a thing or two to us humans.

The Mighty Gorilla

Think gorilla and chances are that you will conjure up images of Tarzan with his gorilla friends or the mighty King Kong wreaking havoc among the skyscrapers of New York. But what is the gorilla actually like as an animal?

Well for one they are the largest primates weighing between 140 and 180 kilograms. Vegetarian by diet, they mainly live in the tropical or sub-tropical forests of Africa where they feed on a plentiful supply of leaves, stems, shoots and other foliage.

They are very close cousins as we share 95 to 99% DNA and are both descendants from a common ancestor. So it follows that they must be highly intelligent. Like us, they have the ability to laugh, feel grief and generally go through the whole gamut of emotions that we can. They have strong family bonds which they nurture and value.

Furthermore, they have the ability to both make and use tools. Some people maintain that they even practice some form of religion! Gorillas from different areas have different types of culture and distinct eating habits! So human-like is their intelligence that they are known to use a stick to gauge the depth of a swamp that they mean to cross.

Gorillas live in groups called groups. These will be led by one dominant adult male and its multiple female partners with whom it will have several offspring. Gorillas are not really threatened by any predator save the leopard who may sometimes get the better of it. It is the job of the dominant male to protect his family and he usually does a very good job of it, to the extent of even laying down his life in the process.

Gorilla babies need the mother to look after them for the first four and five months with the male lending a helping hand in providing them protection and socializing with the younger members of the group. The mothers continue to keep a watchful oversight over the little ones till about 18 to 21 months of age.

Gorillas have a reasonably long life span of between 35 and 40 years of age. Those that reside in zoos even cross the age of fifty. Gorillas use sounds to communicate amongst themselves and there are about two dozen different distinct kinds of vocalizations that they are known to use.

"Hair on a man's chest is thought to denote strength. The gorilla is the most powerful of bipeds and has hair on every place on his body except for his chest."
— Anton Szandor LaVey

Learning from our cousins

We are so genetically close that many of our behavior patterns are remarkably close. Still there are some aspects of the gorilla's behavior which are worthy of emulation by humans. Their social and family bonds, for example, are immensely strong. We could make ours a lot stronger!

The way the male leader of the group of gorillas, known as the silverback, will protect those under its charge, is way ahead of what most humans are capable of. How many of us will give up our lives for the sake of the community? A gorilla is a true knight in shining armor if there ever was one.

Their intelligent assessment of situations and taking the commensurate decisions in light of it is also worthy of emulation. We are so used to the readymade solutions that others provide us that we no longer fully deploy the intelligence that we are blessed with. Everything is taken care of by apps these days! We can all get out there in the real world and see how we fare without the plethora of modern gadgets coming to our rescue.

Perhaps another trait that one could possibly acquire from the gorilla is its vegetarianism. For all its immense size and strength, it subsists only on vegetation. Maybe we could lower our voracious consumption of meat which has spawned this huge industrialization that involves the **harvesting** of living beings that breathe and feel pain like us to feed us.

It might do us a world of good to learn from our genetically close cousin the gorilla, instead of our trying to pass judgment on how clever they can be. God made the earth for all creatures to live together and share its resources. This is something that the animals seem to understand much better than humans.

Our closest relative - The Chimpanzee

The Chimpanzees are absolutely the closest to human beings genetically and, of course, we share a common ancestor. Chimpanzees and we went our separate ways some four to six million years ago.

Being so closely related, it is but obvious that they will display a fair amount of intelligence befitting their status as the most intelligent species in the animal kingdom, besides man. Like man, Chimpanzees have been making and using tools for thousands of years.

They use sophisticated strategies requiring cooperation among individuals to carry out a hunt. They are known to dig for termites with a large stick and then scoop them out with a smaller stick which has been altered for ease of operation.

Chimpanzees use stones as both hammer and anvil to smash nuts to get to the fruit. They are even able to understand human speech and have some rudimentary numerical ability. They can be taught to ride bikes, shoot a gun and even smoke a cigarette.

In the wild chimpanzees, also popularly known as chimps, live in large social groups often numbering in dozens. Like gorillas, they usually walk on all fours but can walk reasonably well on their two feet as well. They can also swing between branches a la Tarzan. They are quite comfortable up in the trees where they can both eat and sleep.

Omnivores like us, chimpanzees mainly feed on fruits and plants, but they also enjoy a feast of insects, eggs, and meat. Female chimpanzees generally give birth to a single infant that rides on its mother's back till the time it's two years old and able to be on its own.

Chimpanzees are about four feet tall when they are upright and weigh between 45 and 55 kgs. They live a long life of forty to fifty years in the wild and are known to even reach sixty in captivity. Like us, the chimps rely more on sight than on a sense of smell. This is facilitated by their bi-focal color vision and depth perception.

The most amazing thing about chimps is the fact that they

are highly altruistic. They will adopt orphaned baby chimps and raise them with the same amount of care that they would lavish on their own offspring. Like humans, chimpanzees possess typical traits of boldness, petulance, stinginess, jealousy and so on. They are emotional like us and can laugh or become sorrowful according to the demands of the situation. Even their hand gestures while communicating are quite similar to those that human children make just before they begin to speak.

This has led to a fierce debate about the feasibility of declaring chimpanzees as aware entities or individuals just like human beings. Perhaps it is their closeness to us as a species that lends the Chimpanzee to being a very popular figure in popular culture. From mass emailing programs like Mailchimp to having them perform in circuses, chimpanzees are a popular cultural figure.

In fact in the US, there is a whole new genre of chimp humor showcased through various popular TV shows like Lancelot and Secret Chimp. As a matter of fact, there is a whole Chimp Channel where chimpanzees dressed as humans are made to mouth lines dubbed by human artists!

"In what terms should we think of these beings, nonhuman yet possessing so very many human-like characteristics? How should we treat them? Surely we should treat them with the same consideration and kindness as we show to other humans; and as we recognize human rights, so too should we recognize the rights of the great apes? Yes."

— Jane Goodall

Chimps and us

There is so much that we can learn from our not-so-distant cousins. Altruism is something that we could learn from chimps big time. Here we have these so-called wild creatures who will adopt orphaned baby chimps and raise them as their own.

Sure humans with their evolved intelligence can be altruistic too, but never at this basic and instinctive level. If that were so, would there be so much inequity in this world? Would the rich nations with their exalted standards of living look the other way while little children in the underdeveloped parts of the world died of hunger, malnutrition and disease?

We could learn to live in harmony with nature from chimps. The chimps live off the forest, but in harmony with it. They take from its resources not in a way that will degrade the forests, but in a way that it continues to be their home. Why they sleep in the trees!

The ability of the chimps to learn from humans is mind-boggling. They have learnt to ride a bike, shoot a gun and smoke a cigarette. They perform stellar parts in our movies and television shows. Can you imagine humans taking so seamlessly to the ways of another species?

Not only do chimps seamlessly adopt our ways, they seem to be having fun while doing so. You need to be a basically empathetic species to be able to pull that one off. Sometimes one wonders if the chimps aren't just humoring a stupid species who think no end of themselves. Seriously, we need to learn empathy from chimpanzees. We should develop the ability to be like one of the animals. That would teach us to live organically in harmony with nature and stop destroying the world with our maniacal ways.

By being so uncannily like us, the chimps teach us that at the core we are animals too and not very different from other members of the animal kingdom. For us to arrogate the right to preside over the destiny of every living animal, we expose the venality of our species.

We decide which part of the world we will commercially develop and which part will be declared a 'protected' reserve for animals. Protected against whom? Against humans of course. This further exposes how hollow our claim of being a superior species really is.

The chimps lead a far more morally upright life. If they are ever aggressive and violent, it is for a reason, not because they can! Though we have something or the other to learn from every member of the animal kingdom, it is the chimp that helps put things in perspective for us, as they share 99% of our DNA.

When the chimps and humans diverged as separate species many millions of years ago, an impartial observer would wonder how the two would shape up. If the same observer were to come across the descendants of the two species today, whom would that person consider a higher species. One wonders.

Today when the world stares at an environmental catastrophe that might eventually lead to an extinction of all forms of life on planet Earth, it is perhaps time for mankind to step back and pause. Material progress is not everything. Like they used to say in the old days - *you cannot eat money.*

By observing the way that our closest relative from the animal kingdom lives its life, we can learn to make a paradigm shift in the way we live our lives to the detriment of life.

To those who would scoff at the idea of learning from chimps, it would do well to remember that a chimp went to space even before the first human being to do so, Yuri Gagarin, earned the distinction. Chimps were sent first to see if humans could survive the rigors of space travel. Yes, that's right! Chimps have been our partners in progress in this world and that.

So it would do us a world of good to learn from an old friend who is also a distant relative. Here's to a lasting partnership between man and the second most important member of the animal kingdom!

He who is cruel to animals becomes hard also in his dealings with men. We can judge the heart of a man by his treatment of animals.
-Immanuel Kant

Orangutan - Person of the forest

Orangutan is yet another species of intelligent primates who impress with their abilities. What characterizes them and differentiates them from other primates is the fact that they spend the maximum amount of time in their favorite habitat - trees. It, therefore, follows that the state of the natural environment would have a very profound bearing on their survival. Perhaps this is the reason why they have been confined to the rain forests of Borneo and Sumatra.

What is special about orangutans as a species is the strong bond that exists between mother and her offspring; exceeded perhaps only by what obtains between a human mother and child. Orangutans depend upon their mothers for as long as ten years, in which time they learn all their life-skills from her - finding food, a place to eat it, the exact way to eat and building a nest to sleep in!

According to members of the Dayak tribe, human beings themselves descended from an orangutan. Perhaps there is some primeval connect that we have with this primate that makes us want to claim kinship! Looking at how popular orangutans are in our modern culture, with the animal finding a prominent place in books and movies, it is not difficult to believe. Good examples of this are the Clint Eastwood starrer, Any Which Way but Loose and the 1996 family comedy Dunstan Checks In.

Baby orangutans, in particular, are quite a hit with people, a fact not lost on advertisers who have used them to sell myriad products. Their intelligence and ability to understand and carry out detailed instructions make them very amenable to human interaction. That notwithstanding they are essentially creatures of the wild, and the forests are where they belong.

In the wild, these animals spend most of the time in the canopy of the rainforest foraging for food. They are quite adept at making tools which they put to different types of use. For example, they will use branches of trees to collect honey, find insects to eat or even deal with insects that sting them! They know how to use leafy branches to protect themselves from rain or sun. They even have a sense of fashion, as they have been observed fashioning a sort of a *poncho* from large leaves which they drape around themselves.

Though omnivorous, these animals largely subsist on spiky foul-smelling fruit. Unlike some other primates, orangutans are solitary animals and fend for themselves. The female of the species may have company though in the shape of one or two babies. The adult male orangutans compete quite aggressively to acquire mates, and it is not uncommon to find some of them nursing serious injuries on account of that.

A fully grown adult orangutan can weigh an imposing 200 pounds, while the female could be one-third to half its weight. They have a fairly reasonable lifespan of about 35 to 40 years. In the past the indigenous people who lived next to the forests inhabited by orangutans desisted from killing these red-haired "people from the forest", for they imagined them to be reclusive people who hid there because they did not want to be used as forced labor.

Present-day people all over the world are far more guided by commercial considerations above everything else, as a result of which the flora and fauna of the various regions of the world suffer depredation. This has resulted in a drastic reduction in the habitat of orangutans leaving them as a highly vulnerable species.

We and Orangutans

You call someone an orangutan and the chances are that they will be highly offended. Who would want to be compared with an orangutan? The fact is that we as a species are a highly arrogant one and have decided that we are the salt of the earth and all the other creatures exist as subservient forms of life.

Nothing could be farther from the truth. It has been scientifically proven that we humans and orangutans are almost 97% similar. We have only evolved differently. While humans degrade and destroy the very environment which sustains them, orangutans derive their sustenance from it in a way that does not harm it. Their life depends upon the renewable produce of the tropical rainforests. They don't consume anything that cannot be replaced. We can certainly learn to live in harmony with nature from the *people of the forest.*

The great bond that an orangutan mother has with its child is something that can even inspire a human mother who herself is so dedicated to the well-being of her offspring. But we have to remember that these are creatures of the wild that eke out a difficult existence in a forest environment where danger lurks at every corner. Yet the orangutan mother will give a decade of her life nurturing her young ones and teaching them life-skills that are so important for their survival.

We could also take inspiration from the fact that orangutans are totally self-dependent. Safety in numbers is not a concept that they believe in. Yet when it comes to fighting for their right to find a mate, the male orangutan will unhesitatingly fight not caring about the consequences. The males of the human species could take a page from the book of their primate cousins and become more self-reliant and depend upon their own resources to get by. At the same time, they should possess the courage of their convictions to fight for their right.

Above everything else orangutans teach us to go about our business and not mess around with other people's business. These animals go about the business of living in a matter of fact way and without any fuss. They keep largely to themselves and don't create a mess in other species' lives. Wish we could do the same.

Tortoise - More than legend

There is something about a tortoise that lends itself to legend and myth-making. Perhaps it is its languorous gait or its hard protective shell into which it conveniently retreats when threatened. It could even be its legendary longevity. They have been around for an incredible 200 million years! One of the most ancient species of animals still extant, it is only apt that it should feature in the creation of legends of American Indians.

In Feng Shui practices too, the tortoise is supposed to be the harbinger of positive energies. It is also used in various religious, magic and voodoo rituals of several cultures around the world. Inarguably the most incredible thing about tortoises from the human perspective is their long life-spans. Tortoises are known to live for as long as 90 to 150 years!

Tortoises are confirmed herbivores and their diet comprises of a variety of vegetation - ferns, grasses, flowers, fruits, etc. Though they appear to have a very slow gait, they can dart when they need to. In size, they range from very small ones that can fit into the palm of a human hand to as big as five feet.

Tortoises need to hibernate in winter and as a preparation they starve themselves! In fact, tortoises are able to stay without food or water for extended periods of time. Perhaps this explains how this animal, which predates mammals and lizards with its hoary history, is such a great survivor.

Tortoises make great pets and children especially adore them. Considering the fact that they live for a very long time indeed, this is one pet you can literally have with yourself for a lifetime.

The popularity of the tortoise in modern popular culture is best represented by Oogway the elderly and wise tortoise, who plays a pivotal role in the blockbuster movie Kungfu Panda. Then there are the popular Teenage Mutant Ninja comics, movies, and TV series. In the past, of course, there was the immortal Aesop's fable about the race between the hare and the tortoise won by the latter on account of its diligence.

Learn from the wily survivor

There surely seems to be some merit in the various legends associated with the tortoise. If it could survive for 200 million years, slow gait and leisurely pace of life and all; surely it gives cause for mankind to pause and think if their relentless pursuit of so-called progress is actually taking them anywhere. Are we likely to survive for 200 million years? Likely not.

It's not for nothing that the ancients in cultures across the world regarded the tortoise as a symbol for wisdom and strength. We could learn to consume less from the tortoise; it subsists on very basic vegetation, and can live without food and water for extended periods of time. Our human lives are driven by avarice - something which invariably brings grief to us.

Like the tortoise, we can learn to live life at a gentler pace. Where is the hurry? We are all one day going to die anyway. At the same time, we don't have to be slothful, just plain diligent. Let us not be the proverbial hare and let our overconfidence cause our downfall.

The tortoise might appear gentle and vulnerable but as we all know, it has the protection of its hard shell to count on in times of danger. We too should have our defenses ever on the ready, even as we go about our business in the most unobtrusive of ways. Truly it makes sense to follow the trail of the tortoise. After all, it has been defined by the wisdom of ages.

Look there goes a Zebra

When you think of an exotic animal, the zebra often comes to mind. A zebra looks like some truant boys did a black and white paint job on a horse. These pretty animals actually are related to the horse and, like the wild horse, herds of zebra roam free in the African grasslands. But unlike horses, zebras have retained their freedom as they don't quite take to domestication.

Among their own kind, the zebras are an extremely social and gregarious kind of animal that love to communicate. They do so by way of whining or barking loudly. Zebras subsist mainly on grass but, if need be, may eat shrubs and even the bark of a tree. They are also blessed with an excellent sense of sight, hearing, smell and taste. That apart, they are a lot sturdier than horses and donkeys, when it comes to resisting pests and diseases.

Their black and white stripes, of course, are their unique sign of distinction and this made them an object of fascination for man ever since he came across this strange looking *horse!* Some Zebras have been used for riding from time to time, but these have been rare instances. All the same wanting to ride a zebra is something that has always attracted a lot of interest in a lot of people.

Various indigenous people of Africa have their own unique legends about how the animal got its stripes. The San folk of Namibia have a legend that holds that the zebra was white to begin with but a fight with a baboon over the right to use a water hole gave it its characteristic black stripes. The stripes occurred when, while fighting, the zebra tripped and fell into a pile of burning sticks.

In modern culture too zebra is often prominently featured, the most prominent example being the movies Madagascar and Racing stripes. It is also a popular motif for furniture and furnishing.

Wish we could be zebras

Why would we envy the zebras - for a host of reasons - their fierce sense of independence for one? For all of man's attempts to get this species under its control like so many others, there has been very little success to show for it. So they are free to roam the extensive grasslands of Africa.

Their excellent faculties include sight, hearing, taste, and smell. Wouldn't we want to be well-endowed in all those departments? Their ability to withstand pests and diseases is another trait we could possess. We are brought down by the puny mosquito!

We could also learn a thing or two about socializing from these funny-looking black and white animals. With all of our social media apps and modern telecommunication, we sometimes don't know who our next-door neighbor is. Maybe that is a lesson to us to jettison all the gadgetry and get down to the basics of talking face to face - just like the zebras.

With all this to learn from the zebra, we found nothing better to do than to call the pedestrian crossings in our modern cities and towns zebra crossing! Perhaps it is just as well, for they do keep the pedestrians safe from being run over.

Isn't it amazing that though most people would never have seen a zebra outside a zoo, it is amongst the most easily recognized animals. Ask any toddler and they will know its name. Perhaps that is indicative of the spirit of the zebra - an animal nobody could tame or closely interact with, yet it happens to be everybody's favorite.

The Mongoose - a hardy customer

Most Indians are familiar with mongoose, thanks to the many stories surrounding the famed enmity between the animal and snakes. In fact, just a couple of generations ago most Indian kids would have witnessed a staged fight between a snake and a mongoose staged by local street performers known as *madaris*, who were snake charmers, circus performers and magicians rolled into one.

The most famous mongoose in the world has to be Rikki-Tikki-Tavi the principal character in a short story of the same name, written by a famous writer, Rudyard Kipling. In it, Rikki-Tikki-Tavi is a brave young mongoose who saves the lives of its family from a krait as well as two cobras. The famous Pokemon franchise which is such a rage with today's youngsters too has a mongoose called Zongoose as a popular character.

For all its ferocity, a mongoose is considered a lucky charm in South Asia and seeing one is considered auspicious. This may be due to the fact that it helps one get rid of rats and snakes. There is also a cultural aspect to it with the mongoose being associated with the Hindu God of wealth Kubera as well as his Buddhist counterpart Vaisravana.

There are many kinds (about 30) of mongooses found in South Asia, Southern Africa and Southern Europe, testifying to their being quite hardy animals. Mongooses are carnivores who eat a varied diet of insects, crabs, birds, lizards, rodents, eggs, etc.

They are very adept at fighting and killing venomous snakes like the cobra because of the fact that they have thick coats and acetylcholine receptors that make them impervious to the deadliest of snake venom. That apart, they are quite agile, which makes them formidable foes of the snakes. Interestingly, though they may be able to kill snake species like the cobra, they never feed on their meat and try not to cross their way, if possible!

Because of their ability to get rid of vermin and fight snakes, mongooses have been kept as pets, and even introduced to lands they are not indigenous too like the West Indies and Hawaii islands, with mixed results. Though they did get rid of the vermin they were overall quite destructive, putting indigenous species at risk!

Some types of mongooses are quite social and live in colonies of about a score members while others are the solitary types. Mongooses live underground and some of them create a network of intricate tunnels or burrows with multiple exits to help them make an escape in times of danger.

Mongoose to emulate

What do we learn from the mongoose? That physical size does not matter. It is the size of your courage that does. Mongooses range in size from 9 to 30 inches, yet they will fearlessly take on deadly snakes like the cobra and the krait and go ahead and kill them. We too can try and punch above our weight, as long as we are agile, nimble and adequately prepared.

Despite their ferociousness, they have somehow been seen as being representative of wealth and prosperity - at least amongst the Hindus and Buddhists. Wouldn't we want to be something like that - aggressive and fierce, yet well-regarded by people as an embodiment of all that is good and prosperous?

Like the mongoose, we too could make our homes safe and secure. Not literally by building multiple exits to escape danger, but in our own way by providing our families with secure homes where they are free to grow and blossom.

All in all, we can learn to be feisty people from this most feisty of animals.

Look! That's a Hippo

Not everybody would have seen a hippopotamus or hippo. Of the ones who have, almost everybody would have seen one in a circus and very few in its natural environment. Irrespective of where one sees the animal, one would most surely be awed by its sight. After all the hippopotamus is the third largest land animal after the elephant and the rhinoceros, weighing a massive 1500kgs. Like the other two large mammals that don't eat meat, the hippo for all its menacing looks is a herbivore feeding on grass!

Though they resemble an oversized pig, the hippos' closest relatives are the whales from whom they diverged 55 million years ago. That explains why they are semi-aquatic, living as they do in the rivers, lakes and swamps of Africa. Their most remarkable physical feature is their enormous mouth which can open to the extent of 150 degrees and easily accommodate a four-foot child inside! The fact that they have huge canine tusks inside their mouths makes them look quite menacing with their mouths fully open.

An animal as imposing as the hippo had to have an impact on the consciousness of the people who came in contact with it, and indeed that happened in their case as well. There is a curious African legend which goes like this –

When God created hippos he wasn't sure where to put them - on land or in water as the newly created hippos clearly wanted. He was worried that with their huge mouths, the hippos would eat up all the fish in the water leaving nothing for the other large animal that loved to be in the water -the crocodile. So God arrived at a compromise solution. The hippos could live in the water but eat no fish. They had to survive on grass instead.

Similarly to the ancient Egyptians, the hippo with its rotund appearance was a female deity personifying pregnancy!

Hippopotamuses largely lead sedentary lifestyles, lazing most of the time in and around water bodies, emerging periodically to graze on grass. Their lifestyle may be sedentary, but the hippos are an aggressive animal, both amongst themselves and with others they may feel threatened by. In fact, they can run faster than humans over short distances!

Hippos live in large groups marked by a hierarchical set-up that is severely put to test where the availability of water and food is scarce. Their numbers in such a case may swell considerably from the ideal group size of about fifteen. As one would expect, the more dominant individuals get to dominate the group.

Hippos have other quite remarkable features like an almost total absence of body hair and their inability to sweat. This causes them to spend a considerably long amount of time cooling off in water or mud. Another unique ability of theirs is the fact that they don't contract any diseases.

What does the hippo have that we don't?

Well for starters, they get to be in the water most of their lives, spending their days either playing in it or in wading across to a grassy bank to have their fill of eating grass. The rest of the day is spent lazing in the mud or a favorite stretch of river or lake - the lifestyle of a true beach bum!

They are strong, don't catch diseases and have no natural enemies. So it follows that they largely lead peaceful and undisturbed life. Don't we wish that our lives were just as sorted?

For all their bulk and fearsome appearance, they don't feed upon any animals to satiate their hunger. For that, they rely solely on grass of which they eat little. This is because their sedentary lifestyle means that they expend very little energy, thereby not needing to eat prodigious quantities like the elephant. We humans could take a leaf from their book and try to lead a similar non-violent and easy going existence.

On a lighter note, if like the hippos, we humans too didn't sweat or have little body hair, we would probably save a fortune on toiletries! Another trait of the hippos that a human being might want to imbibe is the fact that, when under attack, a hippo can fight back very aggressively indeed. We too should have the ability to fiercely protect our interests if they are seriously threatened, no matter how peaceable and non-violent we normally may be.

Nightingale - the Night Songstress

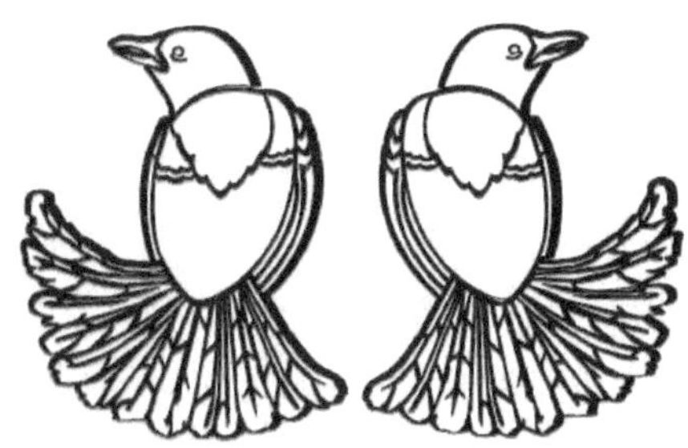

The nightingale has been immortalized by the famous English poet John Keats in his renowned, *Ode to a Nightingale*. The opening stanza of the poem sets the tone for what is an outstanding tribute to this singing bird.

My heart aches, and a drowsy numbness pains
     My sense, as though of hemlock I had drunk,
Or emptied some dull opiate to the drains
     One minute past, and Lethe-wards had sunk:
'Tis not through envy of thy happy lot,
     But being too happy in thine happiness,—
That thou, light-winged Dryad of the trees
     In some melodious plot
Of beechen green, and shadows numberless,
     Singest of summer in full-throated ease.

There has to be something almost otherworldly in the singing of a mere bird that should move a young poet, who died at just 25 to so imbue his poetry with feeling and passion.

The nightingale does not distinguish between day and night when it comes to singing, and this explains the name nightingale, meaning night songstress. The nightingale's proclivity to sing through the night made people believe that it needed no sleep. Consequently, several legends grew around its singing.

One of them has it that a shepherdess who gave many sleepless nights to her fiancé by frequently postponing their wedding was cursed by the latter to turn into a nightingale and forever not be able to sleep! However, the nightingale is considered a good omen by creative people like poets, writers, and singers! In our own country our foremost female singer, Lata Mangeshkar is often referred to as the Nightingale of India. Sarojini Naidu the great freedom fighter and poet was the other eminent Indian woman to be similarly honored.

The most ironical aspect of a nightingale's singing is that though we ascribe a feminine grace to its singing, it is the male of the species that sings - at night to attract a mate and at dawn to mark out its territory! The nightingale is essentially a migratory bird that is found in Europe, South West Asia, and Africa.

For all its legendary singing abilities it has an ordinary and unremarkable brown appearance. The nightingale is basically a shy bird who likes to stay hidden away in some thick bush! It seems it is quite happy to get on with its life that involves feeding on its diet of insects, larvae and berries and breeding when the time is right.

In so far as her singing is concerned this incredibly talented bird with its diverse and complex range of singing, regales us when it deigns the time is right. All we then need to do is listen.

Like the nightingale

Who wouldn't like to be called a nightingale? The fairer sex, in particular, would be quite pleased to be compared to one though we now know that it is the male that does all the singing!

Through the ages, the nightingale has been a source of inspiration to creative and artistic people. If we could similarly be a source of inspiration to others to excel, we would be quite like the nightingale who has received fulsome praise for not only its soulful singing but for being a beacon of hope to lovers, poets, and other artists.

Perhaps the most important lesson that a nightingale provides us is to not make assumptions based on appearances. This bird is nothing to look at but when it comes to singing, it is a powerhouse performer.

Similarly, despite the fact that it possesses extraordinary talent, the nightingale is a shy bird who likes to stay hidden from the eye. Likewise, there may be people in this world who are immensely talented but like to stay away from the limelight. The nightingale teaches us that we could perform for the pure joy of performing, not because we want to receive gushing compliments. Truly this small bird teaches many a lesson to mankind.

Graceful as the Gazelle

A gazelle is the epitome of grace under fire. This small animal is an antelope, native to Africa and Asia the continents that have been chosen by nature to be the repository of the world's wildlife. It has to survive in the ever present shadow of predators like the lion and the cheetah, yet it lives its life as a feisty survivor.

A gazelle may be small, but it makes up for its lack of size, by being very smart and dexterous. Being herbivores they are found grazing on open farmlands that makes them vulnerable to attacks by predators. Their extreme athleticism allows them to sometimes even outmaneuver a cheetah by graceful darting and then turning backward.

Besides, they are forever alert to danger and their excellent eye-sight on account of their large eyes allows them to be always on the lookout. Gazelles live as part of large herds with the males being very aggressive in defending their turf from male interlopers who might come over from other herds. By far the most incredible behavior that a gazelle exhibits is its tendency to jump and bound to showcase its lever of fitness when it notices the presence of a predator nearby.

Their first instinct may be to flee when confronted by a predator such as a lion, but should a member of their herd face attack the older gazelles, both male and female form a circle, lower their horns and make forward to attack it. So they know when it is the time for the flight and when it is for a fight.

The Arabs and the Persians had a special spot of affection for this graceful animal and often gave them a free run of the palace grounds. Many were the poems written and sung in the praise of this graceful animal by their Middle Eastern patrons. In fact, the etymological origin of gazelle is *ghazala* which means a sweet sounding poem in Arabic.

Lessons that the gazelle teaches us

What can we learn from the gazelle? First and foremost is the ability to show grace under fire. A gazelle's life is a constant struggle to survive the deadly attacks that the predators make on them since the day they are born. New-born fawns are often fancied as a meal by vultures who often start circling a spot where female gazelle is about to give birth to a young one. The gazelle not only survives this kind of pressure, but seems to strive in it, using its wit, athleticism, and sheer courage. If we could inculcate even a small part of this kind of guts and glory attitude, we would be heads and shoulders above everybody else.

We can also learn that size is not everything. The gazelle may be a diminutive animal, but it can give a cheetah a run for its money! Can we take on our opponent many times our size and weight, and a killing machine at that? Wouldn't we freeze with fear? Not the gazelle. If it can't flee it will stay and fight along with its friends.

This kind of solidarity for a comrade in mortal danger does not come that instinctively even to us humans. Would we without thinking about our own safety get together to come to the rescue of a member of our group in mortal danger? Some of us might. Others might not.

Wouldn't we also like to possess some of its amazing athleticism and the winsome way which made the ancient Arabs and Persians let them bound along unhindered on their palace grounds? Who wouldn't like to have benefactors like that? How many of us have had the privilege to have been invited to royal or presidential palace grounds?

No Crocodile Tears

The crocodile has received a very bad press on account of that fable about it shedding fake tears. That story does not reflect well about this magnificent beast who is a survivor from the age of the dinosaurs to whom they are related. But that does not mean that they are by any means dim-witted or slow. They are a highly evolved and complex animal boasting of a cerebral cortex and a heart with four chambers.

These aquatic animals are predators par excellence with fine-honed senses that help them detect any movement near them quite easily. They have streamlined bodies and webbed feet, which make them excellent swimmers with the ability to sharply propel themselves forward or make sudden moves in the water. Even on land, they can be very fast over short distances belying their sluggish and lazy appearance.

Armed with powerful jaws and sharp teeth, a crocodile can bite exerting a force of 3000 pounds of pressure per square inch. Crocodiles can grow up to an enormous 6 meters long and weigh as much as 1200 kilograms. What is intriguing is the fact that in all species of crocodile, life starts at about 18 centimeters of length!

Crocodiles are masters of the ambush and prey on fish and land animals that come to the water to drink. They are so good at it that they are known to attack and kill even sharks. Being cold-blooded, they don't need to hunt very often and can do without food for extended periods.

Crocodiles are great survivors and have coexisted with species ranging from dinosaurs to man. Who knows they might still be around when we aren't? In any case, their life-spans are pretty similar to ours with crocodiles living for seventy years on an average. Some even cross hundred!

Crocodiles have always had a somewhat adversarial relationship with humans since the very beginning. Even in present times, they are known to attack and kill hundreds of humans in Asia and Africa every year. It is not surprising, therefore, to find that crocodiles have been feared and sometimes even worshiped by man. The ancient Egyptians for example venerated Sobek a God with the head of a crocodile who protected the people from the dangers present in the River Nile.

The crocodile features in many Hindu legends. In one of them, an elephant devotee of Lord Vishnu has its foot caught in the jaws of a crocodile while bathing in a pond and is saved by the Lord himself who promptly slays the offender. Similarly, in the epic Ramayana the monkey God liberates an apsara (celestial damsel) who had been cursed to be born as a crocodile.

He does that by destroying the crocodile.

So all in all the crocodile has been quite feared by humans and with good reason. That is why most of us are quite happy to steer clear of them!

What do crocs teach us?

Oh plenty! Survivability and longevity above everything. They have been around longer than us, and might yet outlive our species. So to that extent, they are our *gurus.*

Crocodiles teach us what it means to be really feared. There are no species upon the face of this earth that dare tangle with this fierce animal. We might not want to be feared in exactly the same manner, but it would be quite an experience to wield that kind of power over people! The crocodile is a predator like none other with its tough hide, powerful jaws and saw-like teeth. Wouldn't we as professionals in our respective lines of work like to be as efficient and ruthless? Success could be ours for the having.

We could also have some of its enormous strength! With no known natural enemies the crocodile can afford to hunt when it likes and laze around when it likes. In its own way, it lives the life of a king. Which human wouldn't desire that? Last but not the least crocodiles have a healthy life span of a seventy to hundred years! That's a lot similar to ours, but crocodiles don't have to grapple with stress and diabetes!

Jingle Bells, Jingle Bells - Here come the Reindeer!

What image does the word reindeer conjure for you? Chances are that it reminds one of Santa Clause on his sleigh, being pulled by 8 reindeer across the white arctic snow. But surely reindeer do have a life away from the fantasy world of children? Of course, they do, and every bit as exciting. For the unacquainted the reindeer is a large deer that inhabits the arctic regions. It can get to be as big as 4 to 7.25 feet in length and weigh anything between one hundred and twenty to three hundred kilograms.

They live in herds which may vary in number from ten to tens of thousands of reindeer! As would be expected, they are very well-adapted to the harsh environment in which they live. Their coat is brown in summer and changes to grey during the winter and both males and females of the species have their distinctive large antlers which they periodically shed.

Even their hooves change according to season, with their foot pads becoming spongy in the summer when their tundra habitat is wet and spongy and shrinking in winter to enable the hooves to cut into snow and ice. Even their nose helps in warming the air they breathe!

Reindeer migrate over long distances and don't hesitate to swim across lakes and rivers that come on their way, as they are excellent swimmers. The cold and harsh landscape that the arctic tundra is, doesn't offer much choice in terms of food, but the reindeer seem to do quite well surviving on grass, moss, lichen, twigs, herbs and the like. In winter, they will dig into the snow with their hooves to get to their favorite reindeer moss.

They have a superior sense of sight than humans as they are able to see ultraviolet light, the only mammal to have this ability. This enables them to pick out white fur and even urine on the snow, something almost impossible for human beings to achieve.

For reindeer, humans are the only predators, though bears and wolves might target their calves. Human beings inhabiting this stark and cold region have been able to survive only on account of hunting reindeer for their meat. This is not a recent phenomenon but has been going on since the Mesolithic and Neolithic times.

Reindeer meat is today sold across modern retail stores in Scandinavia and the Inuit people of Canada have been using or, shall we say, harvesting the reindeer for everything - food, shelter, clothing and even tools.

In so far as the legends surrounding the reindeer go, Santa's reindeer might be the most well-known one, but they have their origin in an older Celtic tradition involving Herne, the Celtic-horned God. In those days, shrouded in the mists of antiquity dancers would wear reindeer antlers and invoke Herne.

To the tribes inhabiting the Arctic regions of North America, reindeer represented all the virtues of a perfect mother - patience, boundless love and the innate ability to nurture.

Learn from the reindeer

The reindeer have so much to teach us. After all the human populations of the arctic north would have been dead, but for their dependence upon this hardy animal for survival.

So the first thing that they teach us is how to survive in a harsh and inhospitable environment. For all their pride and arrogance, man would not have survived the hunter-gatherer stage or the ice age, if it weren't for the fact that he could depend upon animals to obtain food and other items needed for survival.

The Indian tribes of North America who had an intimate relationship with nature always respected animals that not only provided them food but also taught them how to live in harmony with it. That is why the Inuit people attribute so many wonderful qualities to the reindeer.

Adaptability is another thing that humans can learn from the reindeer. They are completely in sync with their environment - the bitter cold, the lack of vegetation, the paucity of food, the vast snow-fields, the blizzards, the lakes and rivers to cross, et al. Yet they are not fazed and make a life for themselves in that kind of environment.

Finally, we could learn selflessness from this fabulous animal. It gives so much to human beings without getting anything in return. This is quite a unique fact considering that man's survival in the Arctic regions has been entirely on account of the fact that they provided the means for them to obtain food, shelter, clothing, and tools. Mankind owes reindeer a huge debt of gratitude.

Our Debts to Buffaloes

For all the paeans sung in favor of cows, it's the buffalo which provides the bulk of the milk to the vast teeming populations of South Asia. Though cows form a 45% of India's milch animal numbers, their contribution to total milk production is a mere 25%. Buffaloes who constitute 34.6% of India's bovine animal numbers contribute 55

What's more, buffaloes thrive on even low-quality feed like wheat straw, sugarcane tops, and other agricultural residue. Though bullocks are on the whole preferred on account of their being draft animals, buffaloes again are better at lugging loads. Yet it is the cows that are deemed holy in India.

Ironically Mathura district identified so closely with Lord Krishna who was a cowherd in those very parts thousands of years ago, has five times more buffaloes than cows. It is not surprising therefore to discover that those born in the year of the buffalo in the Chinese system of astrology are considered to be very industrious workers!

Buffaloes are mainly of two types - the water buffaloes of Asia who spend a considerable part of their time in swamps and mud and the African variety that live in the forests and grasslands of the continent. There are buffaloes found in North America too, but these are more closely related to European bison than the Asian and African buffaloes.

Buffaloes are essentially herbivores that feed on grass and plants and need to be near water bodies on account of their large intake of water.

These are large animals weighing around fifty pounds at birth and growing up to a size of a thousand pounds in the case of a female and two thousand in the case of males of the species. This is one of the reasons that they are also a vital source of meat for human consumption in Asia.

The buffalo forms a major part of Hindu mythology with Goddess Durga's slaying of the buffalo demon Mahisasura, being commemorated in the Durga Pooja celebrations of Bengal. It is also the mount of the Hindu God of death Yama, and the animal as such is not considered auspicious and is often identified with demons of all kinds. Ritual sacrificing of buffaloes is carried out by Hindus in the Indian state of Bengal and Nepal. So that's quite a complex legacy the buffalo has in India! The North Americans too have their own legends surrounding their buffaloes as their lives revolved around vast herds of the American buffalo that once roamed the North American grasslands.

Learning from the humble buffalo

The buffalo is the unsung hero of planet Earth. Some of the most densely populated nations in the world use it extensively as a milch and a draft animal, slaughter it for its meat, yet not many people are aware of the importance of the animal.

So the first thing that one learns from buffaloes is selflessness and usefulness. If we were to serve society with even a fraction of the kind of selflessness that a buffalo displays, we would be greatly loved and revered indeed. For all their contribution to the human society, most buffaloes have a sell-by date, after which they are sent to the slaughterhouse!

We can learn about hard work from buffaloes. They are useful in so many ways. They provide us with milk and milk products, work as draught animals and when they are done with that they feed humans with their flesh. This is not to suggest that humans should work and contribute till the time of death, but one can surely appreciate one's privileged position and try and contribute as much as one can to the society.

In spite of contributing so much to the well-being of human beings, buffaloes are happy to subsist on the coarsest of feed that mankind deigns to feed it with, unlike the prima donna cows who are not only considered holy and worshipped in countries like India, but also need to be given better feed and taken better care of. If human beings could be similarly uncomplaining and accommodating towards each other, the world would be a much better place indeed.

Lastly, one could learn that looks and one's image don't often point to the true story. The buffalo may not be much to look at and spend its time wallowing in mud, but its usefulness to man perhaps exceeds that of its more glamorous cousin, the cow.

As Ferocious as a Wild Boar

To those who have read the Asterix series of comics, one knows that the importance of the wild boar to the principal characters, especially the giant Obelix is often the high point of the story. Boar is their favorite food, and they would leave no stone unturned to get their hands on one. The animal they hunt is the wild boar which roams the forests of Northern Europe.

Similarly, the wild boar of the Indian jungles, known locally as *jungle sooer* is a feisty animal, quite respected by man and other animals alike for its fierceness. This is one animal whose survival across Asia, Europe, and Africa is not at all a matter of concern, as this hardy animal is known to thrive wherever it is found.

Wild boars are part of a matriarchal society that comprises of related females and their young offspring. Adult wild boars are solitary animals, except for the time when it is the mating season. The wild boar is preyed upon by the grey wolf in most of its habitat, except for the far-east, where the tiger becomes the predator. Mankind has hunted the wild boar for thousands of years and the domesticated pig is descended from it.

The wild boar is a hardy omnivore that consumes a varied diet of fruits, berries, eggs, lizards, mice, leaves, seeds, and so on. It can grow up to be between three and six and a half feet long and weigh between ninety and seven hundred pounds. This animal also possesses tusks which can give it a fierce appearance especially when the males have a go at each other during the mating season.

A nocturnal animal, the wild boar sleeps twelve hours a day and is out and about at night. Quite a self-sufficient animal from quite early on, the young ones known as piglets depend upon their mothers for only a couple of months after which they are ready to be on their own. Wild boars live about ten years in the wild. In captivity they can get to be as old as twenty-five years.

The wild boar, especially a large one can be quite dangerous when attacked and uses its tusks to defend itself. Its thick skin and strong bones make it quite an adversary and fewer animals are more dangerous than an enraged wild boar charging at its adversary. So it was considered quite an act of bravery to be able to kill a wild boar.

In India pig sticking by a group of hunters on horseback is an old tradition that was followed by communities such as the Gujjars and the Rajputs. Indian Royalty and representatives of the British *Raj* too indulged in this sport.

In ancient Persia, hunters would ride on elephant back and drive the wild boars towards marshy land where they would kill them with bows and arrows. In ancient Greece, the boar signified death, as the season to hunt the animals would commence annually in September near the end of the year.

The wild boars were hunted by the Romans and later the medieval Europeans as well. In fact, the French King Phillip IV who had gone on such a hunt died of a fall from horseback while being charged by a wild boar.

Wild Boar for Inspiration

Though human beings have hunted the wild boar for thousands of years, there is much to be learnt from this tough and hardy animal. The first thing to appreciate is the fact that it is a survivor. Through the thousands of years of its existence it has been preyed upon by other wild animals and human beings - yet both its numbers and the size of its habitat have increased.

We humans could learn to similarly thrive in all conditions. Secondly, the wild boar is a hardy and versatile survivor, who will feed on what is readily available. This lets it thrive across different kinds of geographies. Human beings could learn a thing or two about adaptability from wild boars and learn to make the most from whatever is available to them.

Humans could also learn from the wild boars to be more self-reliant. Wild boars become independent of their mothers as early as at two months of age. We humans sometimes don't know what we want from our lives till we reach middle age!

The wild boar is one brave, tough and ferocious customer who will fight till its last breath. Human hunters, past and present, have known and respected this fact. You ignore the wild boar's ability to defend itself at your own peril. We human beings could do with that kind of feisty spirit and the sheer toughness of this remarkable animal.

Lastly, for all the aggression and machismo associated with the wild boar the animal is part of a matriarchal society. Surely we could move a bit in that direction!

Isn't that a Jaguar?

To most people around the world, the Jaguar is the iconic British sports car brand. Most people in India are now aware of this brand as well; thanks to the takeover of the brand by the Indian automobile company Tata Motors.

However, how many of those swooning over the contours of this oh so sleek car are aware of the fact that it is named after a South American big cat, the jaguar? People who recognize the logo of the Jaguar car would probably recognize that it is that of the jaguar - the terror of the South American jungles, grasslands, and scrublands.

If the old world has its fearsome lions, tigers and leopards to be afraid of, the new world has the jaguar. It is the third largest of all feline species after the lion and the leopard and was once found in an area stretching from Argentina in South America all the way up into the Grand Canyon in the United States.

A fearsome predator, it is known to kill a wide variety of prey - deer, snakes, monkeys, turtles, frogs, fish, and whatever else it can manage to lay its paws on! The ability of the jaguar to thrive in all kinds of habitats that encompass deciduous forests, rain forests, swamps, grasslands and mountain scrub probably contributes to their great diversity of diet.

These are solitary animals except at the time of mating and make for fierce hunters. They hunt mostly on ground but are known to climb trees and launch an attack from there. Unlike other big cats, they love water and love spending time swimming, bathing and even catching fish in streams and pools of water.

A male jaguar's territory extends over 19 to 53 square miles which it guards zealously, along with any females that reside there, from other male jaguars. The jaguar may look a little bit like a leopard, but its spots are distinctively dark and the color of its coat can come in many colors -the more common tan and yellow to brown and black.

The jaguar was an important part of the folklore and cultural traditions of the nations and people who populated the regions of Central and South America. To the Aztecs of Mexico, the jaguar signified regal power, magic and war. The best warriors among the Aztecs were known as jaguars. To the Mayans, the animal represented the night and the underworld and in fact, their God of the underworld was personified by the jaguar.

Be like a jaguar

If someone called you a jaguar, chances are that you would grin from ear to ear. After all this animal is a member of the glamorous family of big cats that has lions and tigers as its members. The British marquee car company who made the Jaguar thought the name fit to adorn one of the most iconic cars of all times because the jaguar signified class, power, and royalty.

Not only would most people aspire to be strong and ferocious like the jaguar, but also be as versatile as this big cat. It can attack its prey on land and from a tree, and even catch fish when it wants to. Besides it can thrive in all kinds of topography. Isn't that what makes man such a successful animal (man is an animal!) as well - his versatility and dexterity!

Come to think of it, man does have much in common with the jaguar. No wonder then that the indigenous people of South America identified so much with the animal.

The male jaguar controls a vast swath of territory and defends it and the females contained within it with his all. This is something that the males among human beings would identify with and want to emulate at some level. Unlike its big cat cousins from the old world, the jaguar appears to be a freer animal in what it eats, how it entertains and where it lives. How very new world and American!

Know the Porcupine

The porcupine, though small in size, is amongst the most feared animals. This is because of its unique defense mechanism of using a protective covering of hardened hair called quills which easily come off its skin and get painfully embedded in the skin of any attacker! It is very difficult and painful to remove these quills and often animals that get attacked with these develop infections from their wounds, which can sometimes incapacitate them and even cause them to die - mostly from starvation on account of inability to eat. It is not surprising, therefore, for even predators like the big cats to be cautious around them.

There are about two dozen species of porcupines to be found in Asia, Africa, and the Americas. These animals belong to the rodent family and primarily are herbivores though they may occasionally feed on a lizard. They are found in a variety of habitats that include grasslands, deserts, and forests. The porcupines have a sharp sense of smell, which they put to good use when they set out at night to look for food to eat.

Porcupines have long been part of human legends and there is this particular one from Africa that describes how the porcupine, that originally had a beautiful and luxurious coat of hair, was tricked into acquiring the ugly and hideous quills by a clever jackal that had been highly offended by its vanity.

The American Indians have their own legend about how the porcupine acquired its distinctive quills. Apparently it was once pricked by some thorns of a hawthorn tree and it decided to stick them on its own skin and thereby get protection from predators.

For all its unappealing appearance the porcupine makes it to the dinner table of humans quite frequently in South East Asian countries like Vietnam and sometimes in the West as well.

Anything to learn from the porcupine?

The most important thing to learn from the porcupine is that small doesn't necessarily mean vulnerable. The porcupine is able to give jitters to some of the most fearsome predators known to man, despite its small size.

There are occasions in most of our lives when we get intimidated by our adversaries who seem to be far more powerful and capable than us. Often all that we need to do is to develop a porcupine-like attitude and take them on. Who knows that we may be able to scare off our tormentors by the very act of being brave?

The porcupine is not only very spunky but very hardy and dexterous as well, judging both by the diverse habitat it can survive in and its ability to eat a wide variety of food. Human beings can surely emulate these traits and develop a porcupine-like never-say-die attitude that will see them thrive in all manner of situations.

A porcupine-like reputation would stand any human in good stead as it would make people give you the space you deserve. Who would want to mess with a person who can hurt you really bad like a porcupine? And like the porcupine, if nobody bothers this person, he or she will be a regular sort of person going about their business of living and not really troubling anyone. It sure is a tough customer - the porcupine!

The Donkey - a gem of an animal

You wouldn't call a donkey a gem of an animal, would you? But the fact of the matter is that it is very mean on the part of human beings to treat this animal with disdain if that is indeed what people do. Using this very helpful and hardworking animals' name as a pejorative reflects poorly on us rather than the animal we deem stupid.

Donkeys have helped human beings carry loads for five millennia, and a whopping forty million of these animals continue to do so in the 21st century. Far from being stupid, donkeys are more intelligent than horses in that they will refuse to undertake any task they perceive to be hazardous, no matter how hard its human master tries to persuade it. This is taken as stubbornness or stupidity by human beings but is actually an intelligent act of self-preservation.

To those who have taken the trouble to earn their trust, the donkeys respond quite easily. Not only that; they can be quite playful, affable and eager to learn. It is not surprising, therefore, to find that donkeys are extensively deployed not just as draught animals, but also to lend power to agriculture. This is largely true of the developing world.

In the West they are kept mostly as pets, or may be used to guard sheep. Their presence amongst horses helps to calm the ones who are nervous. The Italians have another use for them - they slaughter donkeys for their meat. The Chinese too consider donkey meat to be quite a delicacy. The Italians and the Chinese seem to have an unlikely food connection with both nations consuming noodles and donkey meat in large quantities! Donkeys have also helped out at the front in conflict zones, carrying equipment and helping rescue the wounded.

They are not too fussy about eating and can quite easily subsist on scrub or by grazing on dry land pasture. This quality of theirs makes them quite invaluable to the many impoverished families who depend upon these animals to help them earn their livelihood. In the long list of favors that donkeys have done to human beings, one can add their services in producing the hard working mules - a product of the mating between a male donkey and a female horse.

Having interacted with human beings for thousands of years, it was inevitable that the donkey would be a part of mankind's folklore. The ancient Egyptians considered it the symbol of the Egyptian sun God Ra. The donkey is an important part of the Biblical tradition with the Old Testament prophesying that the Messiah would come riding a donkey. The New Testament alludes to the fulfillment of this prophecy when Jesus rides into the city of Jerusalem on the back of a donkey. The donkey is the mount of the Hindu Goddess Kalaratri as well.

Unlike many humans, the divine and the holy seem to have no issues in being so prominently associated with donkeys. Perhaps this holds a lesson for us humans.

The virtues of a donkey

Even though one may cringe at being compared to a donkey, but there is indeed everything for man to learn from the humble donkey. It has been selflessly serving man, helping him carry loads, carry out agricultural activities and even serve him at the battle-front. It also makes the ultimate sacrifice of its life to feed man. Above all, it asks for very little in return - just the roughest of grasses and scrub.

If a human being had all of these qualities, he or she would qualify to be a saint. It is only fitting that the donkey be considered good enough to be the mount of divine personages.

The fact that many consider the donkey to be stupid and stubborn only demonstrates the very human tendency to vilify the virtuous. We need to, in fact, smarten up like the donkey and not carry out instructions that might put us in danger.

A donkey is no pushover and will not cooperate with human beings unless an effort is made to earn its trust. These are the traits that would stand humans in good stead.

Understanding the Bat

The bat has been a much-misunderstood mammal and has received some terrible press; thanks to its association with the legend of Count Dracula and also possibly because they are quite often found in old abandoned buildings and ruins. For one to understand this fascinating animal, one needs to rise above one's prejudice and study them with an unbiased eye.

What makes bats unique among mammals is their ability to achieve true and sustained flight. The bats are the second biggest order of mammals comprising of a whopping 1240 species. So for one to brand all bats as blood-sucking vampires is plain foolish. In fact, twenty percent of the bat species survive on fruit. A seventy percent feed on insects and a very small percentage feed on fish or blood of other animals.

Far from being blood-thirst ogres and soldiers of the devil, bats play an important role in pollinating plants and seeds dispersal, so much so that some plant species would die out if the bats were to stop helping in spreading their seeds!

Bats are so primed to take off on a flight that their resting position has them hanging head downwards while clutching a twig or a crack with their clawed feet. Adding to the bizarre imagery is the fact that these are primarily nocturnal creatures often found in dark caves.

They have a perfectly fine vision but they rely mostly on their highly evolved sense of hearing to navigate in the dark. They use echolocation or sonar to detect the presence of objects in their way, much like a radar locates an aircraft. They manage this by emitting high-pitched sounds, which then bounce off objects and carry back information pertaining to their location, size, and distance! You may blind a bat, and it will find its way out of any situation, but if you make it deaf, you have as good as signed its death warrant.

There are innumerable myths and legends surrounding the bat from around the world and many of these are unfortunately negative with even Shakespeare alluding to their role in wicked practices. However, not all cultures consider them inauspicious and the Chinese traditionally believed them to be harbingers of good fortune.

The West with its Dracula baggage has been less than kind to this creature, but this has been largely redeemed by the popularity of Batman, the caped crusader from the fictional Gotham City, who looks up to the bats, and has his costumed ape the look of a bat!

Envious of the bat

What does the bat have that we don't? Oh, quite a few things. Like us, it is a mammal, yet it can fly using its own muscle power. The closest that we can come to that kind of flight is using the hang-glider, but that's not truly self-propelled flight. It just helps you to glide.

We either need bright lights or night vision goggles to see effectively at night. No such problems for the bat. It uses sonar to locate objects in its way. How high tech is that, and how backward are we!

Most importantly, the bat is good for the environment and ecology as it helps pollinate plants and disperse their seeds. We are anything but good for the environment, considering that we usually lay waste to wherever we set up base.

While not suggesting that we take up residence in dark caves and crumbling ruins, we can learn to be more open to others' way of life. Just because bats' lifestyles are so different from ours, it does not follow that they are evil or somehow associated with the devil. Similarly, we could try and understand that different nations and communities have their own way of life and just because that is very different from ours doesn't mean that theirs' is an inferior way of life.

Pretty Penguin

We all love penguins, don't we? They all look so pretty and cute standing erect on their two feet in the vast snows of the Antarctic region. But what are these members of the birds actually like, shorn off their picture postcard imagery?

Well above everything else, Penguins are aquatic birds that spend half their lives in water, to which their bodies are very well-adapted. They are flightless and prefer swimming underwater to feed on their favorite food - krill, fish, squid and other bounties of the sea.

Contrary to popular perceptions, not all penguins live in

Antarctica and several species are found in temperate zones, with one species even living near the equator. The emperor penguin is the biggest of all the species at about 3 and half feet of height, while the smallest, the little blue penguin is only about a foot and four inches tall.

Humans love the Penguins' upright posture and their peculiar waddling gait. These birds seem to be unafraid to approach humans, probably on account of the fact that they have traditionally had no natural land-based predators to fear. That is not the only unique trait that these birds possess. They are able to live in almost freezing temperatures, can dive to a depth of almost 1600 feet. What's more, they can hold their breath for more than 15 minutes. Furthermore, their ability to survive on stored body fat enables them to survive without food for weeks.

Penguins are the most popular bird - period! There is no disputing the fact. It has a lot to do with how they look and carry themselves. Their distinctive shuffle and the fact that they look like they are permanently wearing a tuxedo makes humans take to them instantly. The stupendous popularity of the penguin-themed movie, Happy Feet bears ample testimony to this fact.

It's practically impossible to look at a penguin and feel angry.
-Joe Moore

I wish I were a penguin

We might as well say that, considering just how popular and universally loved penguins are. Wouldn't we humans like to be so dearly loved as well? Then there is the healthy lifestyle penguins lead - living near the sea, going swimming and diving every day and feeding on plenty of fresh fish.

That is an idyllic lifestyle that many of us would give an arm or leg for. Then there are the special abilities that penguins have - of diving hundreds of feet deep, holding their breath for a very long time and most incredibly live off their body fat for weeks. Now that is a set of abilities we humans could do with.

Another adorable personality of penguins is their curiosity towards human beings. They will fearlessly approach human beings and try to find out what they are up to. This is the kind of healthy curiosity that we humans could teach our children to inculcate.

One trait that is observed by most penguin species is monogamy with the male bird preferring to be loyal to a single mate. Now this again is something that many human males could try and emulate!

The most important piece that penguins probably teach humans beings is to live in harmony with nature. Their entire existence and survival depends upon the fragile ecological balance of the coastal areas contiguous or close to Antarctica not being disturbed by human activity. The penguins have been around for sixty million years far far longer than man's 200,000 years. It would be a pity if we became the cause of their disappearance.

Whoever thought that ancient species of animals were all hideous and ferocious, the ever-happy looking and playful penguin belies that and how! Let's all resolve to respect our environment and the flora and fauna around us.

What was that? A Duck-billed Platypus!

It's very odd to look at.   This is the duck-billed platypus of journalism, an egg-laying mammal with fur - it's just something very bizarre
-Jack Shafer

Most of us would have heard of this unique animal inhabiting the continent of Australia that is both a bird and a mammal, from our Geography lessons. It lays eggs like a bird, yet suckles its young like a mammal. When the Europeans first encountered this animal, they thought that somebody has perpetrated a hoax on them - stitching a duck's body onto a beaver-like animal. For them even seeing wasn't believing!

Platypuses are essentially aquatic animals that hunt underwater for food like insects, shellfish, larvae, and worms. Their feet are webbed like a duck's which help them swim quite efficiently. Folds of skin cover their eyes and ears and their nostrils too get sealed enabling these animals to stay submerged for a little while and forage for food with its bill.

They are awkward on land though their webbing does retract exposing nails that enable them to run. Amazingly these animals are the only mammals that are able to receive and deploy electric impulses. This helps them in locating their prey. The wonders of nature never cease!

The platypus defends itself by using its venom-bearing ankle spurs. This venom is strong enough to kill small animals and cause humans excruciating pain. So mess with these animals at your own peril. The platypus was hunted for its fur till about a hundred years ago but is a protected animal these days.

These animals are mostly found in fresh water rivers and ponds, though they live in burrows. It is mostly a nocturnal animal though it does venture out during twilight or under overcast conditions in daytime. The male usually lives within a range of seven kilometers, which will usually also be the home of three to four females.

What can the platypus teach us?

The platypus can, above everything, teach us to respect the tremendous diversity of plants and animals that God has gifted this planet. We need to learn to appreciate that. In a world which is divided along the lines of race, religion, community, gender, sexual orientation and so much else, this unique creature teaches us that there is room for everyone - even those that you may not consider conventional.

What else can the platypus teach us? To dance to our own beat. Here is a mammal that lays eggs, and yet suckles its young! It is as if trying to say, "To hell with convention. I'll live my life the way I see fit."

That is an attitude we humans could do with sometimes. Rather than being dictated to by others, we can decide our own destiny. Then there is its ability to defend itself. Though it is no larger than a house cat, a platypus packs quite a punch by way of its venomous ankle spurs.

We too should possess an innate ability to defend ourselves, so that if anyone tries to browbeat us because they think they are more powerful, they will have a nasty surprise awaiting them. If there were a prize for uniqueness the platypus would win big time. Perhaps this is something else the platypus could inspire us to become - unique and distinctive, not run of the mill and commonplace.

From a scientist's perspective, a platypus is the missing link of evolution that explains the metamorphosis of one type of animal (bird) to another type (mammal). This teaches us that if we search hard enough we will find the evidence to support any rationally thought out theory - like the theory of evolution. Truly the platypus teaches us more about ourselves than any other animal.

A Busy Bee

The bee may be infinitely small, but it plays a very vital role in stabilizing the ecological balance. Any reduction in the number of bees or their absence from an area sends the alarm bells ringing. Bees and mankind have always had close contact as the former make honey - one of the most coveted and delicious food items known to man.

The bees are able to concoct this heavenly sweet syrup from nectar and pollen, which they collect from flowers of plants. In return, they help in the pollination and regeneration of those very plants. If bees are destroyed in large numbers due to pollution and loss of habitat, there would be a massive amount of vegetation loss on account of there being no bees to help pollinate plants.

So bees are of vital importance to us not only for their honey which is renowned for its nutritional and medicinal properties but also because we will lose the vital green cover that plants provide us. Left undisturbed and alone, the bees live highly fruitful and busy lives as part of a massive and complex social hierarchy.

They live in colonies that comprise of thousands of worker bees, males or drones, and a single queen bee. The workers make the intricate nests known as beehives from wax that they secrete from their abdominal glands. These beehives are made of many individual cells which are a repository for pollen and nectar which is food for the developing larvae. The drones' sole purpose of existence is to mate with the queen bee after which they die.

Bees are quite dexterous and adaptable when it comes to facing adversity. They are known to live off stored reserves of food for years in case of adversity! Even in the defense of their homes bees put up a stellar performance. Worker bees will sting the attacker and die in the process, and others of their kind will rush in to take their place.

Bees have so dominated the consciousness of man that these small insects find mention in human rituals and language all over the globe. The English language contains wonderfully evocative expressions like *queen bee, busy bee, making a beeline, having a bee in the bonnet!*

The ancient Sumerians and Egyptians used to mention bees in their poetry thousands of years ago. The Vikings believed that honey made them invincible and the Greeks considered bees to 'the birds of the muses.'

Looking up to the bees

There's everything that human beings can learn from bees. Their perfect hierarchy for example. Each individual knows what they are supposed to do and they dedicate themselves to that task till the very end. A worker bee will work all its life making beehive cells and stocking them with food. When the time comes to defend its home and community, it will do so by giving up its life.

The drones similarly live to ensure the continuity of their community. After they have mated with the queen, they die, as their job is done. The queen bee will be the one who will spearhead the activities of her community who will revolve around them. Most importantly she is the one who reproduces and grows the size of the community.

We humans could learn to work in a similarly organized and coordinated manner for the betterment of mankind instead of fighting wars with each other.

The bees are so industrious and hard working. This is something we could aspire to be ourselves. Then there is their ability to live in full harmony with nature. Their food comes from plants, which they help pollinate in exchange. Their homes are built of materials that come from within their bodies.

Can we humans even begin to approach nature with so much respect and reverence? Not a chance. The bees are able to plan for rough days by storing adequate reserves of food. We humans with our frequent droughts and food shortages could learn a thing or two from bees here.

Lastly, the very presence of bees in an area does it a world of good. The productivity of farms goes up and forests become more lush and thicker. The less said about what the presence of man does, the better! Truly we can't hold a candle to the humble bee when it comes to a host of important things.

The Lemur

What is the lemur? This is a shy and elusive primate that lives on the island of Madagascar. There are an incredible 100 species of this animal to be found there. Some are nocturnal while others venture out during day time. Most lemurs like to stay off the ground and up in the trees, with the exception of the ring-tailed lemur which quite likes sunning itself on the ground.

Amazingly lemurs are a completely matriarchal society with female exercising complete domination over the males, including in the matter of having first right over resources!

Unfortunately because of their distinctively large and luminous eyes and their nocturnal existence, lemurs have been victims of prejudice on the part of humans.

The local Malagasy people traditionally believed lemurs to be harbingers of evil and death. In particular, they felt that if the aye-aye lemur pointed its middle finger at a human being that person was marked for death. This has led to the aye-aye having been almost hunted to extinction.

The fact that these lemurs seem to have no fear of humans and will walk right into a human habitation also arouses the ire and wrath of these people who often kill them on the spot. Perhaps humans should look at lemurs more closely to realize that they are quite a bit like us.

They have opposable thumbs like ours and are found to be more intelligent than our close cousins, the apes when it comes to performing tasks like learning to recognize patterns and even doing some basic arithmetic! If they want to be left to their own devices, we should not grudge them that choice and let them be.

Amazingly the ancestors of the lemurs voyaged to the island of Madagascar on rafts made of vegetation from mainland Africa. That would make them the Christopher Columbus of animals. How can we persecute and destroy animals as smart as that?

Learn from the Lemur

The first thing that one can learn from these remarkable animals is the fact that it takes all kinds to make the world. Just because lemurs look so different, and have apparently strange features doesn't make them alien or evil. In fact, they are a lot more like us than even animals we hold dear like cats and dogs!

That humans are known to persecute and kill such intelligent animals on account of their unfounded prejudices is a monumental tragedy. We should remember that these animals are ancient mariners who traveled on rafts from mainland Africa to the island of Madagascar in a fashion similar to the great human voyages from the old world to the new world.

Like humans, lemurs come in all shapes and sizes, but unlike humans they are not averse to each other and are cross breeding all the time, creating new species in the process. No xenophobia clouds their minds here. The lemurs are one better in their treatment of the female sex as well, giving them the pride of place in their society.

The lemurs do not kill for their food; survive as they do on fruits, leaves, flowers, bark of trees, and sap. Unlike humans, they don't damage the environment and, in fact, depend upon it for their survival. All in all the lemur is a true gem of an animal as bright as the soulful luminosity of its eyes. It is for us humans to clean up our act and stop decimating the environment that supports all life on planet Earth, including ours. All our lives are interdependent and we either learn to live together or we die together.

Wow, that's a Kangaroo!

Children find the kangaroo the most fascinating animal on account of the ability of the females of the species to carry their young in the natural pocket or pouch present on their stomachs. Add to that their ability to stand upright, human-like on their two hind legs along with their peculiar propensity to hop, and you have the template for a very popular animal indeed!

To the whole world and to the country and continent it is found in, the kangaroo is a symbol of the nation of Australia. This peculiar looking animal is the largest of the marsupials - animals whose females carry their young ones in natural pouches on their bodies. The Kangaroo actually comes in a variety of sizes ranging between three to eight feet in height when standing upright and weighing between 40 to 200 pounds.

There are in the main three types of kangaroos though one can count 52 different species found in different parts of Australia. Kangaroos are, as a matter of fact, found in millions in Australia and have generally adapted quite well to the presence of man including the latter's introduction of agriculture to large parts of the country.

This is an amazing animal that is thoroughly acclimatized to surviving in the special set of circumstances that exist on the Australian continent. In times of a drought, for example, a pregnant female can freeze the development of the embryo till as long as it takes to find food!

It further has the ability to manufacture two different types of milk according to the age of two of its offspring (called joeys)! Another amazing ability of kangaroos is that they are practically indefatigable on account of their very powerful legs. These have spring-like muscles that allow kangaroos to hop and move about very efficiently.

Besides they are excellent swimmers which ability comes to their rescue when faced with sudden flash floods, which is quite a common occurrence in Australia. Kangaroos are the most active in the cooler early morning or late in the evening, rather than in daytime when they tend to lie around and chew away on cud.

What's truly incredible about kangaroos is the fact that they have four sets of teeth; when one set wears out from chewing rough grasses another moves in to take its place! They also have very good hearing ability, which they enhance by twitching their ears and determining where the sound is coming from. In summers, they cool themselves by licking their forearms. The evaporating saliva helps cool their bodies.

The kangaroo is integral to any imagery pertaining to Australia. It's part of the Australian coat of arms and is the emblem of the national airline Quantas. Its image is found on some Australian currency notes and the Australian Air Force uses kangaroo imagery as well. The importance of kangaroos in Australian culture is unassailable and preeminent.

What do kangaroos teach us?

Primarily they teach us adaptability and the ability to make oneself one with the environment. If mankind wants to have a secure future, it will need to learn the art of adapting perfectly to the local environment just like the kangaroo is totally suited to the conditions that prevail on the continent of Australia.

The kangaroo also sets a benchmark in the care of their young with mothers carrying their young in their pouches, sometimes for as long as a year. This goes beyond what even human mothers do. Then there is their supreme athleticism that lets them move long distances without tiring. Who wouldn't like to have an efficient pair of powerful legs like these that help one traverse a large distance in one hop?

Their extra sets of teeth are another thing that we could have access to! Lastly very few humans have the fortune to become the symbol of their nation's identity the way the kangaroo has become for Australia. Wouldn't we be happy if we had our image on a currency note? You bet we would mate - as the Aussies would say!

Isn't that a Seal?

Most people don't get to see seals on account of their being marine animals found on remote seashores and icy-floes. Many of us, however, have seen them on TV and are aware of what they look like. Seals have a very sleek and streamlined body and possess webbed digits that act like flippers and help them in moving efficiently in water.

They are excellent divers and swimmers which lets them thrive in the cold and icy marine environment that most seals call home. Seals are a part of the pinniped group of aquatic mammals that are closely related to land-based animals like bears, weasels, raccoons, and skunks.

These are found in the colder regions of the northern and southern hemispheres and spend most of their time out at sea, except when they have to mate, give birth or find safe refuge from predators of the sea like sharks and killer whales.

They themselves mostly feed on fish and shrimp though some of them are known to eat penguins and other seals. An insulating layer of blubber protects these animals from the extreme cold of the environment they live in and they also get similar protection from the fur on their bodies.

There are some eighteen types of seal and some of these are truly massive with the males weighing more than 3855 kilograms and the females a little more than 900 kilograms. The former can be as long as twenty feet while the latter can be around ten feet.

Not all seals are that humongous but they are certainly large. The smallest seal is the ringed seal which is about five feet big and weighs between fifty to seventy kilograms with both sexes being of the same size.

There are a number of interesting legends in the Scottish, Irish and Icelandic tradition about *selkies* - mythical creatures that live as seals in water but assume a human form when on land. This is not really surprising as there are a lot of seals to be found in the waters surrounding these lands and it would be quite easy for somebody looking out towards the sea to imagine that they noticed the metamorphosis of a seal into a human being!

What can seals teach us?

Seals live in a world that is very different from us, but there is always something to learn from all of God's creatures and the seals are no different. The seals' adaptability to cold weather is something that people who live in cold climes could take inspiration from.

Seals are able to maintain a steady and stable body temperature with relative ease, notwithstanding how cold it might be. The natural insulation, that its blubber and fur provide it, is good enough. Compare this with the millions spent on heating and insulation in the cold countries of the world. How the people living there would sometimes wish that didn't have to cover themselves in layers of clothing or have to pay a fortune by way of gas and electricity bills.

The seals are so graceful and athletic in water that it is a joy to observe them. Wouldn't we like to possess this ability to dive, swim and play in the cold and icy waters of our polar regions? But unlike the seals we can only dream about it.

Another thing about seals that humans would understand and appreciate is their tendency to get aggressive when they feel that their young are threatened. They are big and strong enough to attack and kill human beings and have done so in the past.

Human beings, of course, need to be careful around seals as these are wild animals, yet they too would possibly react in a similar violent manner if they perceived a threat to their offspring. Humans would, in any case, be well-inspired to defend what is valuable to them with extreme ferociousness - the way a seal can and often does.

Another one of the apes - Gibbon

There is something about apes that fascinates humans. They are so much like us, yet different, seemingly human and yet totally animal. The gibbons known as the lesser apes are one such animal. They are smaller than the great apes like gorillas, chimpanzees, and orangutans and appear to be more like monkeys in appearance. Yet they are in reality apes and like all apes do not have tails.

Unlike the great apes, however, they do not make nests and also are faithful to one mate, again unlike the great apes. Their movement, that involves swinging from tree to tree, is what really sets them apart as no other animal ape or otherwise comes even close in speed or the distance covered. They can leap an incredible 50 feet at a top speed of 55 kilometers an hour! They can even walk upright on their two legs, but need to raise their arms for balance.

Gibbons are quite a social animal who are not shy of using vocalizations especially when it comes to defending or marking out what they perceive as their territory. They mostly eat a fruit-based diet but can include twigs, leaves, insects and even birds' eggs in their diet, if they lay their hands on them.

Gibbons are found in the tropical rain forests of North Eastern India, Bangladesh, Southern China and Indonesia. Loss of habitat causes the biggest danger to the existence of these animals and efforts are on to preserve their habitats so as to prevent their extinction.

Gibbons were an important part of Chinese arts and literature as there used to be large numbers of these animals found in the Central and Southern parts of the country. There are many references to the animal in Chinese poetry of that time, and a number of the paintings of the era feature gibbons. The Japanese too mention the gibbon in their literature on account of the Chinese influence and their own Zen tradition.

The gibbons and us

What is the most important thing that gibbons inspire us humans to do? It has to be conservation. The gibbons were once found in abundant numbers, but the decimation of their natural habitat by humans has brought them to the brink of extinction. If today gibbons face this threat, the day won't be far when we face the same situation. The time to act is now.

Coming back to more pleasant topics, which man and one

daresay woman would not want to swing between trees the way a gibbon does. Tarzan of the apes could literally learn at the feet of this master when it comes to this kind of locomotion.

One could also ape (pun intended) its healthy diet - mostly fruits and leaves and occasional eggs. How healthy is that? Then there is all that art and culture that this animal has inspired. Wouldn't we want to be featured in poetry, prose, and paintings?

Quite a few human beings are like their fellow great apes - not really faithful to their mates. So there is definitely another lesson some of us could learn from gibbons - that of faithfulness and fidelity.

Lastly a message to those amongst us who are shy and reticent - be vocal about your feelings. The gibbon can't really talk like us yet it uses its mouth when it can to express its feelings! Truly the gibbon is the most fascinating animal and it is a pity that not everybody is aware of its existence or the fact that it faces extinction because of a shrinking habitat. Any attempt that we can make to protect the gibbon would only show us in good light.

What is that huge and colorful bird? It's the Great Indian hornbill

Most people would have seen the great Indian hornbill in a zoo, as it is not a regular run of the mill type of bird. For one, it looks nothing like what most birds do and is really quite large with an enormous bill that is topped by a bright black and yellow casque. It weighs an impressive 8 pounds and grows as tall as 100 to 130 cms. The wing span is an amazing 150 cms!

One can imagine the kind of impression this would create on someone who is seeing the great Indian hornbill for the first time. These birds, as the name suggests, are found on the Indian sub-continent as well as in Indonesia and the Malay Peninsula. These are long-lived birds that notch up an age of 35 years in the wild and about fifty in captivity.

Though primarily subsisting on fruit, the great Indian hornbill will just as well prey on small reptiles, birds, snakes, and mammals. A unique feature of the social life of these birds is that they form monogamous pairs that often stick together for a lifetime. They usually live in groups comprising of anything between two and forty individuals.

These hornbills have a unique nesting ritual that involves the male hornbill collecting pellets of mud, swallowing them and then regurgitating the same material to be used by the female to construct the nest. This is a very laborious process for the male hornbills that are sometimes known to die of sheer exhaustion.

Its impressive size and colorful appearance led to the Great Indian Hornbill being considered an important part of the customs and rituals of certain Naga tribes in India and the aboriginals of Borneo. The former use hornbill feathers to decorate the ritual headgear worn during festivals.

A bird worth envying

If ever there would be a beauty pageant involving birds, the Great Indian Hornbill would surely be among the top contenders with its large size, unique bill and headgear and bright colors. Now, who among us wouldn't want to be considered better looking and more impressive than one's peers?

Not only is this bird good looking, it is a hardworking one too with the male sometimes laying down its life in helping its female counterpart to build a nest. It is a sobering reminder to us human beings that a mere bird can make the ultimate sacrifice for hearth and home!

Then there is the fact that these birds are strictly monogamous and don't desert their mates till the very end. That is something many human beings are totally incapable of.

The Great Indian hornbill is yet another example of the tremendous diversity of life forms found on planet Earth. Just when we come to know of a really exotic species and feel that we have seen it all, along comes another totally different form of life that takes our breath away. Truly if one were to see how talented an artist God is, one really should take time out to try and get to know as many life forms as we can in our own lifetime.

Seeing the Great Indian hornbill in its natural environment has got to be amongst the most fascinating experiences one can have. If one can, one should try and check out this striking looking bird in a bird sanctuary or at least in a zoo.

As far as the Andean Condor flies

The Andean condors are massive birds that fly above the Andes mountain ranges of South America. At ten feet, these birds have the biggest wingspan of all the birds in the world. They weigh up to 15 kilograms and have a body size of about four feet. Because of their enormous size, they perforce have to live in windy mountainous areas so as to be able to fly, taking advantage of the air currents or thermals in the language of meteorology.

Condors belong to the vulture family and are therefore always on the lookout for carrion to feed upon. The choice of food is carcasses of large animals in keeping with their own large size. Their role therefore in cleaning up an area is immense and any dip in the numbers of these birds will have a corresponding negative impact on the local environment. This includes not just the land, but also the sea as they also feed on dead fish and seal. Eggs of birds or young hatchlings are also a part of their diet sometimes.

Condors live long lives - as long as 75 years in captivity and about fifty in the wild. But they reproduce quite slowly giving birth to one chick every other year. Interestingly both parents will take care of their offspring for a whole year.

This condor, which is an indigenous American vulture, is considered very significant culturally to the nations of South America. It is an important national symbol for countries like Argentina, Chile, Bolivia, Columbia, and Ecuador. The bird had a very prominent presence in the cultural lives of the indigenous peoples of the Andean region. In ancient Andean culture, the condor represented the Sun God and was considered the rules of the upper world.

In present times, the image of the condor has been put on the postage stamps of Ecuador, Argentina, Peru, and Chile as well as the currency notes of Columbia and Chile.

Looking up to the Andean condor

The Andean condor plays a vital cleaning up role in the regions that it lives in. Were it not for this, there could possibly be an outbreak of disease in those areas. We humans could borrow a leaf from this high-flying bird's book and similarly attempt to keep our immediate environment clean.

This bird is an excellent parent. It plans its family carefully, and both the parents devote a full year to the rearing of its offspring. We could similarly take a planned approach to parenthood, and afford great care to our offspring to ensure that they are fully prepared for life ahead.

Perhaps the greatest privilege accorded to the Andean condor is its ability to soar above the high Andes mountain ranges riding on thermals. What a view they would be obtaining! What a life! Who wouldn't give an arm or a leg to replicate the experience?

Then there is the cultural significance of the Andean condor. Revered as a representative of the Sun God in the past with an important part in the mythology of the Andean region, it is today a symbol of the nationhood of many South American nations. Which human being holds that kind of an important place in the national consciousness of a whole group of nations? Indeed, there is much to envy about the pride of the South American nations - the Andean condor!

Which Mythical Animal are you?

Our consciousness is influenced not just by what we see around us but to a large extent by our culture and the myths that emanate from it. Many of us may laugh and scoff at those who lay much store by these myths and tradition, but when the brightest human mind of all time, Einstein propounds the theory of relativity which opens a myriad of possibilities in so far as the reality of the universe is concerned, who is anybody to suggest that myths are false and what we see around us real?

Since the dawn of time, mankind has tried to understand the world and his place in it by various ways - art, science and mythology. The world that early man occupied must have seemed a very frightening one with danger lurking everywhere with all kinds of wild animals roaming free and the extreme vagaries of weather against which there was insufficient protection.

To be able to cope with ever-present danger, man must have turned to religion and fantastic myths to find the courage to cope with the daily tribulation. That is how some of the fantastic legends of the world took birth, ultimately leading to the founding of religions which made these legends the cornerstone of their beliefs.

In almost all the religions of the world, particularly the early nature-based religions animals played a very important role. They either represented gods and divine beings or were gods and divine beings themselves. Alternatively, they would serve as a mount of a god or divine person.

Not only were these animals the same as the ones mankind saw around itself, but quite a few of these were mythical or magical. These imagined animals were partly recognizable with features taken from existing animals and partly fantastic. The sphinx, for example, was part human and part lion. Mermaids were half human female and half fish. Then there was the unicorn which was pretty much like a horse, except that it had a horn on its head. The Scandinavian countries had their legends of the selkies - half man and half seal.

In Hinduism, there is Narsimha - half lion, half man - a reincarnation of the Hindu God Vishnu. The ancient Egyptians had Anibus the jackal-headed God of the dead. According to the Muslims, their prophet Mohammad ascended to heaven on a winged-horse known as O Buraq.

Greek mythology has the centaur, the creature with the

torso and arms of a man and the lower body of a horse. The Greeks also had the legend of the Pegasus, the winged beautiful white stallion. In fact, every region and country of the world has its own legends about mythical animals and how they impact human beings.

Man believed in these legends because they comforted him at some level, and he found resonance in the traits of these myriad fantastic creatures. This possibly enabled him to grapple with the amazing challenges that life in those times undoubted presented him with.

It would be interesting to know as to which of these mythical animals we identify most with. The reader would wonder what he or she has in common with these fabled creatures. Let's find out.

Hush, there goes the unicorn

THE UNICORN: The saintly hermit, midway through his prayers stopped suddenly, and raised his eyes to witness the unbelievable: for there before him stood the legendary creature, startling white, that had approached, soundlessly, pleading with his eyes.

— **Rainer Maria Rilke**

The unicorn, a horse-like animal with a horn on its forehead, is amongst the most recognized of mythical animals. Most people would be able to identify one from its picture. Though its legend grew in prominence in Europe of the middle-ages, it was known and recognized by much earlier cultures. Seals bearing the image of the animal have been recovered from the

sites of the five thousand-year-old Indus Valley Civilization in the Indian sub-continent.

In European legends, the unicorn was blessed with some unique abilities by virtue of it having the famous horn on its forehead. It even has a name - alicorn. In the middle ages, there was a great demand for these horns which were supposed to be imbued with special medicinal properties. Unscrupulous elements often sold people fake alicorns that were actually narwhal horns for a neat profit! There are some who say that the legend of the unicorn came into being when European travelers first came across rhinos, with their distinctive horns in the middle of the foreheads.

Because people never actually saw a unicorn, a legend grew around them which stated that a unicorn could never be captured. There was one exception, though. They were known to let their guard down around human virgin females because the latter were pure and virtuous. This often would have fatal consequences for the poor unicorn in question!

It is for this reason that the unicorn is regarded as a symbol of purity, courage and chivalry. Moreover, it is always regarded as a symbol of good and positivity and not as a being inimical to human beings. People believe that it is quite possible for a unicorn-like horned animal to have actually existed in ancient times - not a creature with magical powers, but something that walked this earth in flesh and blood and then became extinct.

There are historical accounts that authoritatively state that the Greek conqueror, Alexander the Great and famous Roman general and warrior Julius Caesar came across the unicorn during the course of their extensive travels. The unicorn has also found a mention in one of the famous Grimms' Fairy Tales, albeit in a negative avatar. There are other famous legends pertaining to unicorns from places as diverse as Jamaica and Mexico!

How does the unicorn inspire you?

Most people would regard the unicorn favorably given its excellent traits though they would find comparison with it a little difficult since this animal is really the stuff of dreams. But still any human being would love to possess some of its traits like nobility, purity of purpose and a chivalrous disposition. In the past, unicorns were often a part of the rituals of heraldry and as such well-regarded by royalty. This again is something any of us would love to be associated with.

Then there is the legendary horn. Though we would not like a horn growing out of our foreheads, we wouldn't mind possessing the legendary powers that it gave to the unicorn. One would also appreciate the fact that the animal is well-disposed towards human beings. If we could be similarly regarded by our fellow men and women, that would make life very pleasant for us indeed.

Take cover, that's a centaur

The famous centaurs of Greek legend with their human head and arms attached to the body of a horse may really have their origin in the Vedic legends of early Hinduism. In any case, the centaurs of Greek legend were cantankerous and troublesome creatures that harassed the human population no end.

The creatures were the very antithesis of the unicorn in that they were vile, evil and generally ill-disposed towards humans. Many even regard a centaur as the devil incarnate.

It is not, therefore, surprising to note then that these weird-looking animals have come to stand for lust, violence, adultery, vengefulness, petulance and plain evil.

Are we anything like the centaurs?

That is a difficult question to answer, as no two individuals are ever the same. However, we all possess the baser qualities which have come to define centaurs. Where we differ from centaurs or do not is in how we are able to rein these in and let our better traits define who we are. In any case, it takes all kinds to make the world!

"Never," said Hagrid irritably, "try an' get a straight answer out of a centaur."
Harry Potter and the Philosopher's stone-JK Rowling

Wow, that's a mermaid

Mermaids, the seductively beautiful creatures with the upper body of a human female and the tail of a fish for its lower body, have inspired the most wistfully romantic and achingly beautiful legends of all times. These ethereally beautiful creatures that are so alluringly beautiful yet unattainable, a lot like us yet so different. Often these stories pertain to a forbidden love between mermaids and humans, mostly with sad outcomes.

There is a legend from the Pacific Islands that informs us that humans have descended from mermaids and somewhere down the line our ancestors evolved and grew a pair of legs and voila - the human race was born!

Mermaids somehow have come to be associated with love in the human mind and it is only fitting that these creatures are sometimes associated with ancient goddesses of love like Aphrodite and Venus.

Another side of mermaids that often comes to the fore is that they are free-spirited and tempestuous and can never be tamed or made to settle down. They are loving, mysterious and alluring at the same time.

Creatures to envy?

There is much to envy about a mermaid - a magical underwater life, complete freedom to be one with nature and the open seas that one veritably owns. When it wants to, it can have a beautiful romantic rendezvous with a human being and then when the time is right, break off the relationship and revert to its carefree lifestyle.

Most humans would love to possess the ethereal and enchanting beauty of mermaids as also their ability to charm their way into the hearts of anyone they desire. We would also love to possess some of the mystique and tempestuousness associated with these creatures. Who likes to have a staid and boring personality?

Lastly wouldn't we like to be the stuff of legends - have books written, poems composed and movies made about us!

"I have heard the mermaids singing, each to each.
I do not think that they will sing to me."
— T.S. Eliot, The Love Song of J. Alfred Prufrock

Behold the sphinx

There are two versions of the sphinx legend - an Eastern one and a Western one. The Eastern one is from Egypt, home to the legendary sphinx statue of Giza. This one has the head of a man and the body of a lion. Sphinxes of this type are benevolent figures and their statues often guarded the entrance of temples in ancient Egypt.

The Western one is the Greek sphinx which has the body of a lion, the wings of a bird and the face of a woman who is considered the very epitome of treachery and evil. Those who have the misfortune of coming across her have to answer a riddle posed by her. If they get it wrong they are devoured by this terrifying creature!

Common to both the sphinxes is the fact that they guard

secrets and to that extent are quite mysterious and intriguing. The Greek version of the sphinx doesn't describe a very happy creature. This was somebody terribly cross with its situation and coming across one was supposed to bring misfortune upon oneself. The Egyptian sphinx, on the other hand, symbolized a host of positive attributes - power, wisdom, enlightenment, and truth.

Would you like to be like the sphinx?

The obvious answer to this probably would be - sure, but an Egyptian one! Like a sphinx, we might like to be the repository of wisdom and enlightenment. We would probably also like to hold and guard the most coveted secrets of all time. Being considered a little mysterious and a bit of a riddle won't do our reputation much harm either. Lastly, we would want everybody in the world to know us as the world famous Egyptian sphinx that every tourist in the world visits!

It's like the riddle of the Sphinx... why are there so many great unmarried women, and no great unmarried men?

   -Sarah Jessica Parker

Is that a selkie?

The selkie legend has its origin in the cold waters of the northern lands of Scotland, Ireland, Norway, and Iceland. This creature is a seal when in water and a human being when on land. The selkies are strikingly good looking with pale skin, green and dark eyes. The females among them are often tricked into marrying human men and even having human children with them. But they always pine to return to their selkie kin and eventually do, leaving misery and heartbreak in their wake.

Selkies are portrayed essentially as kind creatures with large child-like eyes. They have the ability to mate with both humans and selkies and their offspring with the former could either be a selkie or a human. In case of the offspring being a selkie, it will eventually leave its human home along with its mother to go and live in the sea along with others of their kind.

The dark brooding and sea-centric existence of the fisher-folk who inhabit the northern region is quite conducive to creating a legend like that of the selkies and one can well imagine running into one in those parts.

Would you like to be a selkie?

A selkie's life does appear to be an interesting one. Wouldn't some of us humans want to live a double life? One could combine the run of the mill pleasures of human existence with the free-spirited existence of a selkie and its seal companions in the open seas. Then there is the prospect of a cross-species romance that is the stuff of legends!

On a more serious note, selkies are very innocent, trustworthy, kind and loving creatures. Now those are the traits most humans would do well to possess. Then there is their legendary beauty and good looks. Who wouldn't like to have looks to die for?

Probably their most significant trait worth emulating by humans is their loyalty to their own kind and the way of life above everything else. They will go back to where they came from even years after having lived as part of the human society.

As Bob Marley would say - *"If you know your history, you know where you are coming from."*

The Loch Ness Monster

Now this is one monster which hundreds of people claim to have seen and some have even apparently photographed it, but as no scientific evidence of it actually existing has been conclusively presented, it remains a mythical creature.

The Loch Ness monster dubbed Nessie on account of the lake Ness (Loch Means Lake in Scottish) in Scotland where it was first spotted in modern times in 1933, has since become a fascinating legend. There have been intermittent reports of its sightings right up to present times and the frequency of these might suggest that the creature might actually exist!

It purportedly has a long slender neck, a horse-like head and a couple of humps on its back. Nessie is apparently quite large measuring anything between fifteen to forty feet in length and weighing about two thousand five hundred pounds.

Though the creation of this legend is a largely twentieth-century phenomenon, there are reports that there were sightings reported as far back as the sixth century! The amazing thing is that people have even taken pictures of the monster, and there is a report of sonar waves having detected its presence in the waters of the huge lake, but there has been no scientific corroboration.

This hasn't stopped the spawning of a huge tourism industry built around the Loch Ness monster Nessie legend. This monster marketing phenomenon has doubtless been a boon to the local economy of the region, with tourists trooping in from all parts of the world to possibly record their very own personal sighting.

A legend like Nessie

There are many among us who aspire to be famous like Nessie in every corner of the world. Add to that a certain mystery, allure, and danger and you have the makings of a true blue legend. There are some people who would possibly want to tantalize the world like the Loch Ness monster does. It wouldn't be a lot off the mark to call it the Greta Garbo of monsters!

Possibly the biggest takeaway of the Loch Ness monster, which is lost in all the hoopla surrounding it, is the fact that this creature values its privacy. You may catch a fleeting sight, but it will not care to fraternize with you. It may be a tourism rockstar to the entire world, but all that it cares for is to live its life on its own terms in the depths of the Loch Ness.

Yeti-the elusive snowman

The legend of yeti, the elusive snowman from the high Himalayan regions mirrors that of the Loch Ness monster in many ways. Here again is a creature that has been sighted many times, but whose existence is yet to be proved. But that hasn't done anything to dim the popularity of this creature which has even found mention in one of the Tintin comic books.

The yeti is supposed to be a large ape-like creature that walks on its two legs in an upright position, like a human being. It is supposedly quite tall with some accounts describing him as being as big as ten feet. A thick coat of fur protects it from the extreme Himalayan weather and though it does not move very fast because of its size, it is quite stealthy and manages to disappear quite easily. It is also reputed to have superhuman strength.

The yeti is also known to use large rocks as a weapon to defend itself if threatened. It apparently can hurl these with devastating force. There are tales in the Himalayan region which allude to its ability to communicate telepathically. There are others who say that it communicates by whistling.

The legend of the yeti has been around for hundreds of years if not thousands and the role of the local mountain folk in it is immense as they had a story-telling tradition about the yeti. From the 19th century onwards, a number of westerners came into contact with people who claimed to have come in contact with the yeti. This led to the yeti achieving worldwide fame.

Soon enough there were reports of people having seen the yeti's footprints, hair, and even excreta! Others reported seeing the creature itself. Like Nessie, the Yeti too has become a cultural phenomenon. Often referred to by the appellation, *The Abominable Monster*, the yeti too might have become a tourism draw, but for the fact that it chooses to live in some of the most inhospitable and inaccessible regions of the world.

Be like the yeti?

Not many people would like to be anything like the wild scraggy creature that lives in the high Himalayan mountainous regions, yet the yeti is a huge legend. So there must be something about the alleged lifestyle of this mythical animal that appeals to us at some level.

The very fact that it chose the icy wastes of the high Himalayan region as its home intrigues us about the yeti. Then there is the whole mystique about whether it actually exists or is just a figment of some oxygen-starved Himalayan shepherd's imagination!

The elusive nature of this beast tells us of a creature who is either very shy or values its privacy above everything else. Now these are the traits that we can identify with very well. There is also the fact that the yeti has been described as an ape or sometimes even human-like creature. This naturally ups the level of curiosity about the yeti. *Is it possible that the yeti is actually a human being albeit of a different kind?*

Lastly, the yeti is a celebrity! Now that is something about the yeti most humans would unequivocally want for themselves. Be that as it may, the legend of the yeti is not dying in a hurry - at least not until the time that the snows still fall on the high Himalayan passes.

Ever seen a griffin?

The griffin is a mythical creature that has an eagle's head and a lion's body. It is supposedly imbued with special powers in that its feathers can cure blindness and its claws can help detect poison by changing color. Predictably this led to a racket in the old days involving the sale of fake griffin parts where antelope horns or ostrich eggs were respectively sold as griffin claws and griffin eggs to superstitious folks.

Most of the legends surrounding the griffin describe it as

a stately creature that conducts itself with courage and grace. They are also renowned for their intelligence as also dedication to their mate. Griffins would never take another mate if their own dies. They are also known to be attracted to gold and, therefore, are often found guarding treasures.

Griffins formed an important part of the art of the ancient Babylonians and Assyrians. They form a part of Greek and Roman mythology as well. Additionally, these creatures find a mention in Grimms' Fairy Tales where they are portrayed as being inimical to humans, but full of wisdom and knowledge, nevertheless.

A griffin-like person

Would one like to be compared to a griffin? Probably so. Though it is often represented as a fierce and terrifying creature, its qualities of bravery, intelligence and allegiance to its mate are quite worthy of emulation.

Besides a griffin is nothing, if it is not royal and stately. That is something quite a few of us would aspire to be. Most mythical creatures like the griffin are very complex creatures that have some good and some bad in them. In deciding whether they are worthy of emulation or not, one needs to look at the overall package. By that yardstick, the griffin certainly passes muster.

Rising the phoenix

Who hasn't heard of the term, *rising from the ashes like the phoenix?* The phoenix is a mythical bird that apparently has the ability to resurrect itself even after it has burnt to ashes and died.

This is the story behind the proverb which alludes to a person's ability to resurrect himself or herself from the most adverse of situations. For the ancient Egyptians and Greeks, the phoenix represented the Sun God. The dominant legend surrounding the phoenix says that there can only ever be one and only phoenix. Every five hundred years it builds a nest of twigs and sits in it waiting for the rays of the sun to set it afire. The fire burns the bird to ashes from which a new phoenix arises to live for another five hundred years!

This mythical bird is used as an emblem on the flag of the both the county and city of San Francisco. In any case, the bird is the most potent symbol of resilience and resurrection known to man. It is not surprising that there is a city by that name and even a brand of shoes in India.

Rising from the ashes like a phoenix

We all know the proverb and what it stands for. We would all like to be like the phoenix and possess the ability to resurrect ourselves again and again and again. The phoenix inspires us to strive for all that is good and beautiful and believe in the promise of a better life.

If we can go about living our lives purposefully till the very end while believing that one will get a second shot at life and a third one and so on, we would probably never experience much sadness in life. The Hindu philosophy of *karma* is a bit like this. You get any number of chances to redeem yourself.

Of all the mythical creatures, the phoenix is the most

sublime and ethereal one. For one, it is a regular bird, albeit a magical one and does not possess any grotesque features like other mythical creatures sometimes do. If anything, the phoenix is a bird that presents you with a philosophy of life.

Did you see the Pegasus?

Pegasus, the winged white stallion, has its origin in Greek mythology. Legend has it that it carries the thunderbolt of the Greek God Zeus. By some accounts, Zeus is the father of Pegasus.

Greek legend has it that there was no one who could tame Pegasus, save a classical Greek hero Bellerophon who had to prove himself worthy of the task by spending a night at the temple of Goddess Athena. He eventually persevered and was able to ride it. Pegasus itself was no less persevering when it flew to the heavens, Bellerophon astride his back. The jealous gods sent a gadfly to sting it, but all that it resulted in was in throwing the rider back to earth while Pegasus managed to reach its destination. It is therefore also said that Pegasus denotes perseverance as much as it denotes a quest for higher things.

This beautiful pristine white animal is the leitmotif of much of the Greek art of antiquity. To the ancient Greeks, the flight of the Pegasus had its parallel in the human soul's quest for immortality. Even today the Pegasus is a potent symbol of aspiration and is often used as a brand name or logo by leading corporate organizations around the world.

Like a Pegasus? Oh yes.

The Pegasus as a symbol has a lot of positivity attached to it. It inspires one to excel and achieve higher objectives in life through dedication and perseverance. At the same time, it is also a symbol of beauty and grace with its pristine white body and graceful bearing.

Most people would readily like to be associated with this legendary creature that according to Greek mythology was the offspring of Zeus the king of gods. Besides this is one mythical creature that is good to look at and won't send shivers down your spine with its grotesque body parts and features!

Quite a dragon that!

The dragon has been a hugely important part of two civilizations that are otherwise distinctly different. Europe and China may have been at the opposing ends of the cultural spectrum, but they both have had very similar looking creatures assume a very central part in their cultural narrative - the dragon!

The dragon is a reptile-like creature which every so often breathes out fire! It is believed that dragons may have their origins in peoples' contact with hissing cobras or crocodiles - hence the association of danger with dragons.

The major difference in the narratives of the Chinese and European dragon is the fact that in the former the dragon is regarded as an auspicious symbol depicting power while in the European narrative it has more often than not been cast as a villain.

For the Chinese, the dragon is a potent representation of all that is great about their culture and it completely dominates their art by way of imagery. Chinese Emperors would proudly claim that dragon blood flowed in their veins! It is also one of the important sun signs in the Chinese Zodiac. The year of the dragon repeats itself in a twelve-year cycle - the last one having fallen in 2012.

In Europe, of course, the dragons were seen more as a problem than anything else. St. Patrick the patron saint of Ireland is credited with having driven dragons out of the country.

The blessings of the dragon

In the Eastern tradition, the dragon is a creature you would like to be associated with for it is considered to be a harbinger of good tidings! After all, it was the symbol of the emperor himself.

It was supposed to possess great wisdom and could bestow great blessings on those that it favored. At the same time, it had the power to create the seasons and this prompted the farming community to pray to it so as to ensure a bountiful harvest.

One wouldn't really be averse to being given so much importance, would one? So one might quite fancy the idea of being a dragon, but in a country like China, where the people would fall over each other to curry favor with you. Besides it would feel great to be considered the harbinger of great fortune and the maker of weather.

There are people who are quite dragon-like in that they are very regal in their bearing and have an impact on the lives of those who are associated with them. Their very presence makes people feel good about themselves.

On the other hand, there may be some people who are like the European dragon - feared and reviled, with the people wanting to keep them at an arm's length. It's funny how the same creature can be perceived so differently by different kinds of people.

What on earth is that? An elf!

An elf is a small humanoid with long ears and a cantankerous nature. An important part of Norse and specifically Icelandic legends, stories about the elves have been doing the rounds for centuries. The funny thing is that there are still some people who believe in their existence and have actually claimed to have sighted them. Prominent among them is Icelandic pianist Erla Stefansdottir who actually organizes elf sighting tours!

The elves are considered the last of a race of semi-divine beings or people who preceded the human race and were very closely connected with animals and nature. There is, of course, the Christian connection of elves in the tale of Santa Clause who is helped by a number of brightly dressed elves. They help him in various ways like making toys for distribution to small children for Christmas and taking care of his reindeer. Elves feature prominently in the works of the twentieth-century fantasy writer JRR Tolkien. Prominent among these are the novels, *The Hobbit* and *Lord of the Rings.* Elves were also featured in Poul Anderson's *The Broken Sword.*

On the whole, the elves are perceived as being quite

mischievous and given to interfering in human matters with rather negative consequences for the latter. Their ability to use magic makes matters even worse! They would, however, on some occasion be helpful to human beings as well.

There was on the whole quite a bit of ambivalence about people's attitude towards elves in Europe of the old days, where the legends of these beings originated. They were regarded as quite good to look at, and not above using their charms to seduce human beings! Another way by which they could harm humans was by causing them to fall ill.

Then there were the tales of elves who would help people. There is a famous poem by August Kopisch which describes how while the lazy people of the German city of Cologne slept, elves take upon themselves the responsibility of helping finish the work of the people like carpenters, bakers, butchers, winemakers, and tailors.

Be an elf? Why not?

The elves seem to have all the fun. Not only do they have magical powers, they apparently are immortal as well! Then there are their famed good looks and their ability to have people do their bidding.

They may be naughty and capricious at times, but they are also known to help humans, and sometimes even saints. St. Nicholas (Santa Clause) himself would vouch for that! On the whole, exchanging one's life with that of an elf might be a lot of fun. They may be mischievous and troublesome at times but they do make up for it with their good deeds. Besides human beings are far from perfect themselves. They would make very good elves themselves.

The Indian *Rakshasas*

Indian mythology is replete with tales of rakshasas or demons who largely personified evil and led lives of sin. Tales from famous Indian epics like the Ramayana and Mahabharata, as also the scriptures like the Puranas are full of tales of evil rakshasa, also known as asuras who would often have run-ins with the gods or devas.

In most cases the supreme gods of Hinduism, Shiva or Vishnu would have to assume human form to destroy these evil personages and restore order to earth and the heavens. Rakshasas like Ravana, Kansa, Hirnukashyap and many more are an integral part of Hindu folklore and known to most.

What is remarkable about these tales is that they paint a much-nuanced picture of these troubled souls, often providing a rationale for their behavior. Some of the rakshasas are actually divine beings who were cursed by the gods on account of some grave transgression and by becoming rakshasas they would inevitably get killed by the hand of one of the gods and thereby achieve salvation.

Often the Rakshasas were less villains and more the victims of a power struggle between them and the gods; with the latter often resorting to unfair means to get the better of them. Some of the rakshasas were great scholars and devotees of one of the major Hindu gods. Ravana is a prime example. He was not only a great ruler but a scholar as well as ardent devotee of Lord Shiva. His own brother Vibishna was a devotee of his arch rival,

Lord Rama the human reincarnation of Lord Rama.

Are you a rakshasa?

The term is a pejorative in India, given its association with the biggest villains of Hinduism. But a close study of these tales would teach us that the idea behind these is to let us know that we have both kinds of tendencies within us - those of the righteous devas and the devilish asuras. It is up to us as to which traits we suppress and which ones we cultivate.

At the same time, we are taught that there is no absolute good or absolute bad in this world. Both the gods and the demons have their virtues and weaknesses. This nuanced look at people's motives and intentions is a gift of the Indian nation to the world. There is no black and white in this universe. The truth lies somewhere in between. We are all both devas and rakshasas.

Gandharvas - know one at your own peril!

The Indian religions of Hinduism and Buddhism are a vast treasure trove of myths and legends. Prominent among these are the ones associated with Gandharvas. These are male celestial beings and consorts of the heavenly Apsaras their female counterparts

The Gandharvas are known to be adept at the arts, particularly singing. They are often depicted as carrying messages between the gods and humans. Often depicted in humans or part animal shape, they are blessed with magical powers that let them fly and even live in the scent of flowers and the bark and sap of a tree!

In the heavens, they are given the duties of singing and guarding Somrasa, the celestial liquor! Under ancient Hindu law, a consenting male and female could enter into a Gandharva marriage, without having to undergo a ceremony of any sort. The connection of Gandharvas with music is also brought to the fore in that many renowned musicians of the traditional classical genre are known as Gandharvas.

Be a Gandharva. Yes, please!

Being a Gandharva would really be a male fantasy come alive. Who wouldn't want to be one? You get to marry the divinely beautiful apsaras, fly through the air and live as ether in the scent of a flower or the bark of a tree!

You are a great singer too and get to guard the famed Somrasa! What's more, you find mention in the holy books of two of the greatest religions in the world - Hinduism and Buddhism.

The Jinns - they are around you

We have discussed many a mythical creatures that are a part of the Christian, Hindu, and Buddhist traditions. The Muslims too have their own mystical beings and none is more all-pervasive than the jinns.

The jinns are an invisible form of life created by God to live amongst us, undetected and unknown. They are neither strictly human or animal, but a separate class of their own. According to the Quran, the jinns were created from smokeless fire and were free of the constraints of time and space, unlike mankind that has to respect these limits. They are therefore blessed with the power to move very quickly indeed.

Jinns are also blessed with great magical powers which they can use to come to the aid of human beings. The most famous jinn of all times has to be the one who came out of Alladin's lamp! As we are well-aware, that particular gentleman could perform wondrous miracles at Alladin's bidding.

The creation of the jinns apparently predates that of humans. Like human beings there are good jinns and bad jinns. The good ones help mankind come closer to God while the bad ones would take them to the devil.

Jinns, though living among us, have their favorite places of residence. These include old abandoned buildings, cemeteries and the places where animals are kept. They are also to be found in places where money transactions take place (perhaps they are present everywhere!)

Would one like to be a jinn? No, thank you, sir.

The jinns being spirits, it is doubtful that any human being would want to be one. But they sure would want their abilities - superhuman strength, great speed, agility and the power to perform miracles.

They would also surely want to possess the jinns' ability to not be constrained by time and space. Then there is the advantage of invisibility. These jinns sound more like characters from Marvel Comics than anything else. Maybe big Hollywood studios should take note!

Who's that naughty child? Oh God, that's a goblin!

Goblins are elf-like creatures that are short in stature, have long ears and play horrible pranks on people. Not very nice people, if they can be even called that, they are known to be destructive, yet weak and cowardly when confronted.

Most of us are familiar with the wicked ways of goblins, thanks to the Noddy series of books by Enid Blyton, as also the Harry Potter books written by JK Rowling. Known to eat just about anything, they are not above consuming human flesh, which they actually consider a rare delicacy!

As a society, goblins are quick to produce offspring but are not able to engage in much productive work to support their families. So they take to stealing from human beings whenever they can. As they are too weak to defend their homes from attacks by stronger beings, they inevitably end up living in the most remote and unlikely of locations.

They treat their young abominably often keeping them in cages as pets. They view all other living beings as food and are not averse to eating the flesh of their own kind!

Getting inspired by the goblins? No way!

As there are hardly any redeeming features in goblins, it is hard to see how they could inspire human beings. Perhaps the better ones among them like the elderly benefactor of Noddy in the books by Blyton could be someone you could look up to.

We could possibly give them some marks for the tenacity with which they try to make a life of their miserable existence, given their circumstances. If we are in a charitable mood, we might give them a mark or two for their legendary mischievousness.

A banshee's wail

The banshee is a female spirit whose appearance is the harbinger of someone's death. This legend has its origins in old Irish mythology. A banshee's most prominent act is to start wailing in anticipation of someone's impending death.

Though a legend of superstition, as is usually the case, many people believe in the existence of banshees. Right through history, there have been claims of people having seen banshees and the last such sighting was reported not very long ago - in 1948.

The origin of this legend probably lies in the old Irish tradition of ceremonial mourning by certain classes of Irish women. With the passage of time, some women were thought to possess the ability to know when a person would die and would commence the wailing, even when the person in question was alive (poor soul)!

The banshee woman acquired sinister overtones with time. She was no longer human but a spirit and her appearance became quite scary -withered old hags wearing black or grey garments and combing their hair with a silver comb. Sometimes, however, they would appear as bewitching young women. They could also appear in the shape of animals, usually associated with witchcraft, like weasels, hares, and hooded crows.

What can you learn from banshees?

What the banshees can teach us is that everyone who lives has to die some day and we should be ready to face that possibility. Perhaps in their fierce mourning they provide us with a catharsis, for aren't there times in everyone's life when we want to cry out loud. The banshees carry out that task for us (even if it is only in myth) and provide us with the much-needed release.

Bar-Yuchnei

If all the major religions of the world have to have their own mythical creatures, how can the ancient religion of Judaism not make a contribution to the list? So here we present the bar yuchnei, a colossal bird whose wingspan could shut out the light of the sun.

Once when it threw one of its eggs down on the ground below, there was hell to pay! Apparently 300 cedar trees were destroyed and sixty villages got flooded.

Perhaps as just punishment, it was prophesied that the bird would be roasted on the occasion of the coming of the Messiah and all the righteous Jews would partake of it in a banquet! Wow. Talk about poetic justice!

Learn from the bird

Should we envy the gigantic bar yuchnei? Perhaps for its ability to be able to block the sun! People in countries like India would probably want to requisition the services of this bird in reducing exposure to the scorching summer sun.

Then there is the sheer power of the bird to wreak destruction on planet earth. Imagine destroying sixty villages with your eggs. Maybe armies around the world should raise a few battalions of these super birds!

Lastly, there is the take away that no matter how high and mighty you are, there will be a time when you will get your just desserts, just like the bar yuchenei which will be roasted when the Messiah comes. So enjoy your power while it lasts, but do not forget that like all good things, that too will come to an end.

Beware the Leviathan

This is another one of the monsters from the Jewish tradition, albeit much better known than the bar yuchnei. This is a large sea monster and the word used to describe it has become a regular one in the English language and is used to denote anything that is massive (usually large sea creatures like the whales).

Leviathan is, in fact, also a word in the modern Hebrew language and it means whale! According to Jewish tradition, however, the Leviathan is a huge sea-based dragon that will, like the bar yucheni, be slaughtered and offered to the righteous to eat when the Messiah makes an appearance!

What me leviathan?

The leviathan is a word much used in literature. To that extent one wouldn't mind being associated with it - also the fact that it has made its way into the lexicons of two languages.

Where one would like to keep a safe distance from this animal is on the day the Messiah makes an appearance. Who wants to be slaughtered and fed to a whole lot of people who are in the mood to party?

Stay clear of the werewolf

The legend of the werewolf has taken hold of the imagination of the Western world like nothing else has and there are innumerable books, tv shows and movies that have been made on the subject. A werewolf is essentially a special kind of human being who has the ability to shapeshift into a fearsome wolf and this usually happens on a full moon night.

This ancient folklore probably has its origin in people infected with rabies because of dog bite behaving weirdly because of the effects of the disease. But for writers this whole concept has become a godsend, imagine a normal human being by the day who gets the urge to become this very fierce and dangerous wolf by the night. The possibilities for drama and intrigue are immense.

Werewolves may have become the holy grail (ironically) of the Gothic pop literature of the twentieth century, but the fact of the matter is that people in the middle ages believed in the concept and along with that of witches! A lot of innocent people were put to trial in those terrible times, accused of witchcraft and werewolvery.

Would you like to be a werewolf? Maybe!

Considering that most people don't believe in werewolves anymore and these as creatures are only useful in helping myriad writers and filmmakers to create content for entertainment, there is no harm in imagining oneself to be a werewolf and getting kicked about it.

As a werewolf you could embark on an adventure every night and get away from your staid office job, or whatever it is that you do for a living. You may be a boring family man by day and a wild carnivore roaming freely in the jungles by night. Think about it. Sounds like fun!

Hisss - there goes the Ichadari Naag

The ichadhari nag is the Indian equivalent of the Western werewolf legend. This is essentially a shape-shifting male snake that can assume human shape at will. Like in the West, this creature has become the leitmotif for countless Bollywood blockbusters!

Apart from being an efficient shape-shifter the ichadhari naag is in the possession of a precious gem nagmani, which is even more valuable than a diamond. Every so often unscrupulous humans would kill an ichadari naag and steal the coveted nagmani little realizing that the picture of the assailant has been captured in the pupils of the dead snake's eyes.

It is now left to the shape-shifting ichadari nagin, the wife of the ichadari nag to use this evidence to stalk and destroy the killer! One can imagine why the Indian filmmakers so love this legend.

Me an ichadahari nag?

Well considering that you can live your life both as a human being and a snake, you would get to experience two kinds of lives. Besides you would be a rich person as you would possess the nagmani.

If someone rubbed you the wrong way, you could promptly assume the shape of a serpent and have your revenge. Besides you might even sell the rights of your story to a Bollywood film producer.

Steer clear of Orthus the two-headed dog

Orthus is amongst the most feared of the mythical animals. This is fierce two-headed dog that forms an important part of Greek mythology. He was owned by the three bodied monster Geryon and it was his duty to guard his master's herd of red cattle on an island in the Mediterranean Sea.

This was a very fierce animal indeed and greatly feared by all. He was eventually killed by the famous Greek hero, Hercules, who was required to herd away the red cattle as the completion of one of his famed ten labors.

Inspiration

The only possible inspiration that one can draw from a character such as Orthus is the creature's faithfulness to its master. It does lay down its life to that end.

Garuda - Lord Vishnu's favorite bird

Garuda is a large bird that essentially serves as a mount of the Hindu Supreme God Vishnu. It also forms part of many Buddhist legends. India is not the only country with a claim on this special bird. It is an important part of the cultures of other nations like Indonesia, Thailand, Mongolia and Surinam.

Garuda is the sworn enemy of the mythical naga race of serpent people. It is for this reason that the image of a garuda is often worn as an amulet to protect one from snakes and snakebite.

Garuda finds prominent mention in the great Hindu epic, the Mahabharata which describes in detail the circumstances surrounding its birth and achieving immortality. Garuda has similar significance in Buddhist mythology as well.

This bird is an important cultural symbol for India and South-East Asia with its statues and other representations being a common occurrence. The Indian Air Force has an elite special forces unit called the Garuda Commando Force while the Indonesian national airline goes by the name Garuda.

Divine like Garuda

Garuda is a divine bird, the vehicle of Lord Vishnu himself and a symbol of auspiciousness. It has many nations of the world revering it and according it a place of pride as the national symbol.

Who wouldn't want to possess some of its traits? It says something about the culture of the nations of the East that they vest so much goodness and power even in animals and birds.

On its part, Garuda inspires us to strive and attain what might appear beyond our grasp.

If a mere bird could make the gods themselves sit up and take notice of its prowess and accord it the status of immortality, we as humans are capable of so much more. Above everything else, the Garuda teaches us to be ambitious, brave, audacious, and strong. Nothing will come between us and the success we deserve if we make ourselves strong as Garuda.

In this section of the book, we studied the impact of mythical animals on the collective human consciousness. The reason that all human civilizations have their fair share of mythical animals lies in a couple of facts. The first is that there is a bewilderingly large number of animal species on earth, each stranger than the other and it must have been very difficult for early man to process all this information leave alone understand it.

So what mankind didn't understand, it fashioned within the confines of its own imagination. Crocodiles and snakes became dragons, and people suffering from the ill-effects of a dog bite became werewolves. The second reason behind the spawning of these legends really has to do with man's early attempts at understanding creation. The mythologies of the early Greek, Roman and Hindu civilization is replete with stories of mythical animals that played a part in the affairs of gods and men.

One thing which stands out is that since antiquity mankind has known that animals and mankind have much more that joins them than divides them. The advent and spread of Christianity, which placed man above other animals, marked a break from this long held tradition.

It is not until Darwin propounded his theory of evolution

and the origin of the species that this seamless link between all forms of life came center stage once again. This was a return to the earlier dispensation when the linkages between humans and animals were much stronger.

Humans, who in the early millennia of their existence were either hunters or farmers, depended largely upon animals for their survival and interacted with them all the time. It was but natural for them to have developed myths and legends about them.

Through these myths, they sometimes assuaged their fear of the unknown and at other times they used them to put in place ceremonial rituals that would bring order to the community. So if in today's times we sometimes scoff at the fantastic nature and sheer absurdity of some of these legends, we should for a moment put ourselves in the shoes of our cavemen ancestors for whom a bolt of lightning from the skies that sets a forest ablaze may very plausibly be the handiwork of the sky-dragon who spits fire!

It is the myths of a culture that lead to the formation of its religion, art literature, science, and philosophy. Animals, both real and mythical, help vastly in the creation of myths, as these provide man with the means to articulate his beliefs. Because we have been hearing these myths right from the very early days of man's existence on earth, we can instantly relate to stories of these mythical animals, whichever part of the world they might originate in.

We still feel a primeval thrill whenever we are told of such legends. That is why we throng to the cinema to watch movies of the Harry Porter franchise or Lord of the Rings.

That is also why werewolf stories and vampire tales fascinate twenty-first century teenagers as much as they would have their counterparts in the middle ages.

Lying at the bottom of our fascination with the animal kingdom is the fact that we are an integral part of it. The fact that we have come to be the dominant species at this point in time does not mean that this is how things will always remain. We are actually no more than just one species, in a long line of animals that have done their dance and retired into oblivion.